RETURN TO VIETNAM

T H E   M E M O R I E S

Stan Bain

Inquiries and Book Orders should be addressed to:

Great Writers Media
Email: info@greatwritersmedia.com
Phone: 877-600-5469

ISBN: 978-1-959493-74-7 (sc)
ISBN: 978-1-959493-73-0 (ebk)

DEDICATION

I dedicate this book to those Vietnam veterans who have or still are struggling with memories that haunt them daily. I hope sharing my experience in returning to Vietnam will give them ideas that maybe they can consider returning to the scene where their thoughts were manifested.

ACKNOWLEDGMENTS

First, my cousin Greg Bain and his wife, Clare LaMeres. Without them, this trip would not have been possible. They supported me in sponsoring this trip that would change my life; they will always have a special place in my heart. Thank you.

Also, Mr. Giang, our tour guide, made this trip special. He was the best of the best tour guides one could ever have for visiting Vietnam. Throughout the trip, his knowledge and history of the areas we visited made those places even more enjoyable. He constantly researched and tried to find an orphanage that was the focus of this trip. The story of his harrowing ordeal after North Vietnam invaded the South made this trip even more exceptional.

Our driver, Mr. Ky, professionally weaved us through traffic that would terrify most people; he performed like a choreographer.

Elyssa Fernandes of Audley Travel, and her staff, worked over several months to put together a tour that tried to meet our needs. Her interest in my original book and assistance in marketing it is greatly appreciated.

Finally, a special thanks to the Vietnamese for being so gracious and welcoming veterans to their country. We were met with smiles and kindness at almost every place we visited—whether it was museums, businesses, or hotels.

CHAPTER 1

Beginning The Trip

It was November 3, 2019, at 0400 hours. I was standing at the curb in front of Delta Airlines at Orlando International Airport. The air was fresh from the night rain, and the palm trees swayed from a light breeze—a contrast to the pine trees in Montana. My thoughts wandered back to October 2018, to my hometown—Kalispell, Montana. I had a book signing on my first book, "You Are Never Alone," and it was during that book signing that several people asked if I would ever want to go back and visit those areas that had the most effect on me. "Yes, I would like to go back," I told them, knowing darn good and well that wasn't anything I would be able to afford any time soon.

Fast forward one year, and here I was, about to embark on a trip to Vietnam to rediscover those places that had such a tremendous impact on my life. I didn't have a clue how this trip would affect me—the people I would meet, the changes to the landscape, or the many surprises along the way. I was hoping to understand better the Vietnam War and how the Vietnamese people survived to make their country a fast-growing travel destination. And I was also hoping to understand better the events that had so dramatically transformed the optimistic and fearless young man I had once been into the haunted and troubled veteran I had become.

CHAPTER 2

How It Started

The day after my first book signing in October 2018, I stopped by my cousin Greg's office. We hadn't had much time to chat the day before, and I wanted a chance to catch up. "I was listening to you yesterday while you were talking about your book," he said. "The questions were interesting, but I noticed when they asked you about going back to Vietnam, you said you couldn't afford to."

"Yes," I said, "it's beyond my capability, at least for now. One nice lady gave me $60 toward the trip," I said, "which was great, but I'm still about $10,000–12,000 short." We both laughed.

"My dad never talked about his experience in World War II," Greg said, his tone serious. "I knew from Mom he had flashbacks and memories of that War, and he *had* mentioned wanting to return to the Philippines, but that never happened." I nodded but said nothing. "I understand more about Vietnam from your book," he said, "and I think it's important that you return."

"Well…" I said, "a trip like that would be off in the future."

"No, you don't understand. I want you to start planning that trip. Clare and I will go with you and pay for everything."

I looked at him in disbelief. "Did I hear you right?"

"Go ahead and get the process started," he said. "Figure out what places you want to visit and pick some dates, and we'll make it happen. That's the least I can do. I couldn't help my dad, but I *can* help make your dream come true."

I was speechless. "But let's try *not* to go in the rainy season," he said.

"Yes, and maybe not the hottest months either," I added.

And that's how it started. I left his office feeling like I had just won the lottery and spent the flight back refining my list of must-sees for the trip. When I returned to Florida, I immediately checked with a travel service, and they contacted me with their overseas agent, who did not leave a favorable impression. While several different tours to Vietnam were available, none covered areas of interest. I made several more phone calls and discovered that Audley Travel made custom arrangements for several locations worldwide. Elyssa Fernandes, a Thailand and Vietnam Senior Specialist was our chief contact. Finally, after numerous e-mails and phone conference calls between Greg, Elyssa, and myself, the Vietnam portion of our trip came together. Clare worked with Elyssa on picking the hotels. Clare also arranged the airline part of the trip.

We decided to leave for Ho Chi Minh City (Saigon) on November 5, 2019, from Los Angeles International Airport (LAX) and return to the States on November 19, 2019. We would travel to several locations that were significant to me and including a short cruise down the Mekong River. The only location that was iffy was the orphanage. The people on the ground in Vietnam weren't having much luck locating the facility.

CHAPTER 3

Orlando to Los Angeles International Airport—November 3, 2019

I was up early, having slept poorly the night before while thinking about the upcoming trip. I kept wondering if this was really happening and if it wasn't something I had conjured up and convinced myself was real. The fact that several other people were involved and that the ticket agent at the Delta desk treated me like a regular passenger bolstered my confidence. She smiled when I put my bag on the scale and handed her my ID.

"I see you're going to LAX," she said. "Vacationing in California?"

"No, Ma'am," I said. "Heading to Saigon."

"I only have your reservation to LAX," she said, double-checking the computer screen, "returning here on the 19th."

"That's correct," I said. "Other parties made my arrangements for the Saigon part, and we'll be overnighting before going on to Saigon tomorrow."

"Sounds like a nice trip," she said. "I see your hat says you're a Vietnam veteran. Going back to visit someone?" she asked.

"Yes," I said. "My demons, among other things."

"Wow! Well, you have a safe trip, and I wish you well," she said as I reached for my carry-on and turned to leave. "And thank you for your service," she added.

"Thank you, ma'am," I said. "You have a nice day."

The Orlando airport uses trams to move passengers from ticketing to departure terminals. It's all very efficient. I went through security and caught the train to the assigned concourse and, once there, stopped at a coffee shop as it was still 0'dark thirty, meaning the sun had not come up yet. I then proceeded to the gate with so many thoughts going through my head; it was hard to sort them out. With forty minutes to boarding, I called home to touch base one more time. Clare had arranged seat assignments in business class for this direct five-hour flight. It was a luxury that I could really appreciate.

My flight arrived in LA on time, about an hour before Greg and Clare were scheduled to arrive from Montana. I picked up my bag and waited for them in baggage claim. While there, I met a young couple in their fifties who were going on a cruise. We chatted about their voyage and my trip as well. It was a pleasant visit that helped to pass the time.

I spotted Greg and Clare, hugged them, and we grabbed our bags. We headed up the escalator to catch a shuttle to the Hyatt Hotel. We got to the hotel mid-morning, so the room wasn't ready yet, but we were able to check our bags and catch an Uber to the Manhattan Pier. When the Uber driver dropped us off, a cop on a bicycle came over and gave him a $55 ticket for stopping where he did. That was a bunch of crap! Clare shared the drive money to cover the fine. We walked around enjoying the sights, as tourists do and marveled at how calm the ocean was. Few people were on the beach, and only a few were swimming or trying to surf on the small waves. We found a corner restaurant by the pier and had lunch before returning to the hotel in mid-afternoon.

After getting checked in and settled, we met in the hospitality room for a drink. By the time we finished dinner, we had called it a night, knowing the next day would begin the experience I'll never forget. I don't think I slept at all that night. I thought about where I was heading again and wondered how different it would be this time. Rather than packed into a military aircraft with a bunch of recruits destined for Pleiku, Vietnam, this time, I'd be traveling first-class on a commercial jet with my cousin and his wife, heading to Saigon.

CHAPTER 4

LAX to Tokyo—November 4, 2019

We left the Hyatt around 8 a.m. as we had to be at LAX three hours before our flight departed. Check-in went quickly, and we took the escalator toward our concourse. As we stepped on the moving stairs, Clare got tangled up in her suitcase and twisted her leg. Despite the pain, she limped along, although she would continue hurting for the first few days of the trip. We stopped at the club lounge for a snack and drink before our flight, which was already an hour late.

We boarded the All Nippon Airways (ANA) Boeing 787-9 Dreamliner, and each had our cubicle in business class. The seat could be used as a recliner or a bed and came with our pair of slippers and a TV. The service was excellent, and we didn't want anything—the only way to travel on a twelve-hour flight. The Japanese flight attendants were all the same height and shape, wore the same hair style, and looked like Quintuplets. They even changed their outfits when they served food and drinks during the flight.

Author's Photo Collection
Clare, Myself, Greg aboard Boeing 787-9 Dreamliner

The flight was comfortable, but I didn't sleep much. Mostly I just dozed and thought about the trip ahead. Would I be able to visit my old bases? Was the orphanage still standing? Were there kids living there? Would I find what I was looking for? That was unclear to me, but I was hoping for peace from the pass. I needed to find the orphanage. To me, that was an essential part of this trip. If you are no longer there, then at least see the location. Best yet, if I could locate any of the nuns who worked there. I may find out what happened to the kids after I left Vietnam. But it's been fifty years, be a snowball's chance in hell of ever happening. I knew my expectations were more significant than I could honestly hope for. What I gain from this trip will come to me when I return home.

During the flight, Clare had problems walking due to the escalator mishap. One of the flight attendants noticed and arranged for a wheelchair in Tokyo as our time between flights would be short, and our connecting flight to Saigon departed from a different concourse.

We landed in Tokyo a few minutes ahead of schedule. Greg and I took off to the proper concourse while Clare was taken by wheelchair on a shortcut to meet us there. As it turned out, Greg and I got lost; the signs were confusing, and we ended up outside the security area. Thanks to a flight attendant's help, we were directed to the correct concourse but had to re-enter through security to get to it and the gate. I stopped at a restroom near the entrance, and when I finally caught up with Greg, he said Clare was already on board. That was good news as we were a little stressed.

CHAPTER 5

Ho Chi Minh City (Saigon)—
November 5, 2019

It was a five-hour flight to Saigon, our entry into Vietnam. Many thoughts again started to immerge about my daily images and what I may experience during my tour, how I may react, etc. I tried to relax, had a drink, maybe two, sat back, and tried to sleep. However, the images in my head were a full-time attack—thinking about the soldier I killed and finding a picture of his wife and his baby still branded in my brain, seeing the kids in the orphanage in excruciating pain and ending their suffering. I sat back up and ordered another drink (reader beginning to think there was a lot of drinking on this trip; YES, you could say that) and closed my eyes, trying to think of the good times in Vietnam; yes, there were many. The Vietnamese people I met, and that it being a beautiful country that I knew would be a tourist destination someday, are only a couple. Anxiety began to set in during the last hour before landing in Saigon. I felt clammy and had shortness of breath. We kept circling due to rain and traffic. I broke out into a sweat. God, are we ever going to get on the ground? I felt like my life was crashing in on me, like an elephant was sitting on me. I got up and reached for my carry-on and took out my aspirin bottle; the only thing I had I thought would calm me down.

The flight attendant came over and asked, "Sir, can I help? You Ok?"

"Yes," I said, "I could use some water."

She brought me a water bottle and helped me put my carry-on back in the overhead bin.

"Thank you for the water," I said.

I took a couple of aspirin, lay back in my chair, closed my eyes, took deep breaths, and tried to relax, thinking of fun things like scuba diving in cresting water around beautiful reefs. We circled several more times. I was beginning to feel better and breathing normally again. And by the time we landed, I was a calm, cool Vietnam vet.

It seemed like it took forever for us to taxi to the gate. Finally! We disembarked around 9:30 p.m. and were directed to customs. There were several lanes; we got into the first lane to show our passports and visa. The customs officers appeared to be all military. Greg and Clare were in front of me and went right through the line with no problems. My turn. The officer was about thirty and looked like he was not having a good day. He took my passport and visa. He looked at me and said, "remove your hat!" which was the same Vietnam Vet hat I had been thanked for my service at LAX!

I removed my Vietnam Vet hat that had several service pins on it. I thought this wasn't an excellent way to start this trip. After a few seconds, he said, "there is a problem with your visa, and the documents are not complete. You have to go to the visa line to reapply." I took my passport and visa from him; we glared at each other, and I left to go to the visa line. I glanced at Greg and shrugged my shoulders like I didn't have a clue…

I stood in the visa line, put my hat back on, and was a little ticked off because I knew my documents were good. I worried about having to apply for a new visa. Greg and Clare were on the other side, and I couldn't talk to them. After a few minutes, I was waved forward. The visa officer was Vietnamese. I gave him my visa and said, "the officer at that passport line told me that I had to re-apply."

He was dressed in plain cloths and was a much older gentleman and asked, "give me your documents." He looked at my visa, shook his head, and said, "there is nothing wrong with it."

He turned my visa over, stamped and signed it, and then returned the visa to me.

"Go back to the customs line," he said.

At first, I was tempted to get into a different lane; however, I got into the same lane I was in before. I walked up, gave the officer my passport and signed visa, and stood at attention, removing my hat.

He glared at me, I glared right back at him, and he gave me my passport and visa back and waved me on. He didn't say anything.

Still at attention, I put my hat back on, did a right face, and marched off. Under my breath, I mumbled, "Kiss My Ass," hoping he didn't hear me.

I caught up with Greg when he asked, "What happened?"

"Oh, I guess the idiot didn't like my hat and wanted to give me a little gruff about it," I said.

We met Clare in the baggage area, grabbed our bags, and walked out into this huge waiting crowd, many holding placards with their clients' names. We walked toward the curb and saw a young gentleman holding a placard with "Audley" and my name.

"There's our man," Greg said. We waved and walked over to him.

"Hi! My name is Tom." He was tall and thin, looked in his twenties, a Vietnamese, and spoke excellent English. "I work for Audley, and my job is to escort you to your private vehicle so we can go to your hotel."

As we walked to the vehicle—a nice Toyota that appeared to be new with two rows of seats behind the driver, giving us a lot of room. Tom said, "This is your driver. His name is Ky (*pronounced Key*); Ky was a little shorter than me, around 5 feet 6 inches and maybe mid-thirties, and also Vietnamese. "He will be your driver while you're here in Vietnam. Your tour guide and Interpreter will meet you in the lobby at the hotel on Thursday at 9 a.m."

We exchanged *HI*'s with Ky and shook hands. He smiled and bowed his head before loading our bags and ushering us up into the van.

"Does Ky speak English?" I asked Tom.

Ky spoke up, "Little bit. Not much."

We laughed, knowing now he does understand English.

Author's Photo Collection
Caravelle Hotel Saigon

As we drove through Saigon to our hotel, which took about thirty minutes, we asked Tom what he had done. He said, "I'm going to school to become a tour guide. I enjoy talking to people and know the area, so I want to build my own tour guide business someday. Your hotel, the Caravelle Hotel Saigon, is a famous hotel and very much part of the Vietnam War history. During the 1960s, the Caravelle Hotel Saigon was the home of the Australian and New Zealand Embassies and housed TV bureaus like NBC, ABC, and CBS, which played an information role in the Vietnam War. War Correspondents met at the end of the day in the Sky Bar with a drink, shared their stories, and watched the war bombs at a distance.

Tom asked, "Mr. Bain, what year were you here in Vietnam?"

I said, "I arrived in June 1967."

Tom said, "Don't know if you knew that on August 25, 1964, around mid-day, a bomb exploded on the fifth floor where the journalists stayed. Fortunately, they were all on assignments. Several rooms were damaged, and there were no fatalities. Assume the Viet Cong (VC) had much to do with it."

Tom paused and said something to Ky about the traffic, I think. Tom continued, "after the fall of Saigon in 1975, the government took over the hotel and renamed Independence Hotel until 1998 when the hotel was refurbished, and the local investors reestablished Caravelle Hotel. The hotel was also famous for a movie called The Quiet American, starring Michael Caine in 2002."

Tom continued, "the hotel was remolded, including an additional twenty-four-story tower, and increased the hotel into 335 elegant guest rooms with an outdoor swimming pool and bar. They provide two contemporary fine dining restaurants and the Saigon Sky Bar with a view overlooking the Saigon city skyline."

After dodging traffic which was an entanglement of trucks and motor bikes, I asked Tom, "is traffic always like this?

"No," Tom said. "The traffic is pretty light this time of the day."

Oh, I thought it did not look light to me. We arrived at our hotel. As the van drove up to the front door, we were met by several hotel personnel. We thanked Tom and told Ky we would see him on Thursday.

We were escorted through the lobby to the front desk. We received a pleasant greeting from several staff members, and one of them asked for our passports. It did not take long to get checked in and get off to our rooms. We agreed we meet in the lobby in fifteen minutes and search out the Sky Bar. It was around 1 a.m.

I walked into my room; the spacious and luxurious setting took me; I did not expect to have such accommodation in Vietnam. Right away, I saw a small sign on the desk warn that tap water was not drinkable. This sign would become a familiar site throughout our journey.

I put a few things away and headed to the lobby to meet Greg and Clare. We met up and headed to the elevator marked Sky Bar. The elevator was small, and we were joined by a gentleman and two ladies wearing short, revealing dresses. The route included a short walk up steep stairs to the bar's entrance. Poor Clare, not to be left behind, limped up the stairs and was more than ready for a drink once we made it. It was a nice bar, but a little noisy due to the live band. The view of Saigon at night was stunning, with the lights from traffic and buildings. I could not get over how much it had changed from my last visit. But it had been over fifty years, and I was there only a few hours.

Author's Photo Collection
Sky Bar overlooking Saigon at night

We ordered drinks and some snacks and tried to unwind from the long trip. We enjoyed the view. The bar was open with a series of French doors on two sides and fresh air from light rain. The smell of the fresh rain was sweet; you could hear the traffic down below. After our drinks, we sat back and enjoyed a relaxing atmosphere. Looking around, I noticed several ladies; I looked at Greg, and he smiled, "working girls?" He asked.

"Yeah, that's what I would also say," I said.

Clare had been relaxing, looking around, and taking in the scent of the air, sipping on her drink. "What are you guys talking about?"

We chuckled, "Oh, just the view," I said.

"Yes, it is a nice view from up here looking out at the lights illuminating Saigon," she said. "I bet you could hear bombs off in the distance and sounds of the War from here during the sixties.

I'm sure she also noticed and guessed the ladies in the bar were prostitutes.

After a few drinks, the fatigue finally caught up, and we headed to our rooms. We agreed to meet in the hotel lobby at about 8 a.m.

CHAPTER 6

Saigon—November 6, 2019

Our first day in Saigon was spent adjusting to the time change and doing some light sightseeing. We all felt kind of drugged and weren't too eager to do a lot of running around. We met in the hotel lobby as agreed and decided to go to the restaurant for what was an excellent buffet of American, Asian, European, and British foods. The services were amazing, and the restaurant was comfortable. While there, we took some time to review the options before us.

"What you guys like to do today?" I asked.

"Thinking we will take a walk around the area, maybe couple blocks, and see what's close by," Greg said.

"Sounds like a good plan," I said. "Maybe a dip in the pool later."

"How about we meet in the lobby in about fifteen minutes and head out?" Greg said.

"Sounds good," I said. "See you then."

After breakfast, we prepared to leave. Greg an I talked about which way to go while Clare—ever the adventurer—took off down the street. We followed like sheep, although Greg has these long legs, so he easily outpaced us.

It was a pleasant walk, with several clothing shops from Europe, jewelry shops from many countries, perfume shops from France, and several street vendors selling food, handmade jewelry, and carved figurines out of wood. Some sold maps and paintings of Saigon, local rivers, and sunsets. Most were beautifully done. And pretty much a variety of souvenirs was available.

There was construction going on down the block, with several buildings in various stages of remodeling. Greg and I found their methods interesting as we were contractors in the United States. They used lots of human resources carrying materials up ladders, even though several heavy equipment tools were available. It seemed the workers didn't have the knowledge on how best to utilize them as the tools sat unused on the job site.

During lunch breaks, workers gathered around the various sidewalk vendors selling the standard noodles or rice with chicken or fish broth. They would sit in little tiny chairs like we would have back in the United States used for little children. Sometimes people would squat down and sit on their heels. If I tried that, it would take two workers and a horse to get me up! All the while, the street vendors scurried around cooking to continue their business.

I stopped by a model ship builder. I couldn't believe the detail of his work. For many of his Buccaneer ships, the cannon door would open, and the cannon would slide out. The sails, mast and yard arms, and cleats were so detailed with ropes and supporting details that they seemed almost natural. The ship builder didn't have any fancy tools; I only saw knives, files, needles, and various paint brushes, but there were no power tools. He also made Japanese sailing junkets. Amazing artist. I would have loved to own one of his ships, but I live in an RV and hardly have room for my couple of sailing ships, three-inch and twelve-inch boats. But then I probably couldn't afford the shipping either. Still, it's something more to add to my bucket list.

We walked several more blocks and noticed other buildings were also being remodeled. Even well-known hotels like the Hyatt and Sheraton were getting face lifts. Suddenly, Greg stopped and looked around. "Stan, did you notice how all these workers are doing construction, but there aren't any toilets?"

Author's Photo Collection
Model Ship Builder, near our hotel

"Ah, yeah," I said, "that is strange nowadays, the businesses around here don't seem to have restroom signs, and I don't see any public areas either." We walked on, thinking we needed to watch our step.

I said, "During the War, while walking around in towns, you would see that many restrooms were public, that is, there were no stalls that I remember, but had toilets and trenches on the floor you would pee in, or women would squat over, and the person next to you could be a woman. But when you go, who cares; besides, you may learn something from the person next to you. I chuckled.

A couple of days later, driving down the road, Clare said, "look, that guy is taking a pee along the road!" Well.... I thought that answered the question about no toilets.

As we walked along, a young kid, maybe nine or ten, kept following me, trying to give me a shoeshine. "They're tennis shoes,"

I said. "They don't need a shine." But he insisted; I was going to have a shoeshine. He won and had my tennis shoes shined. Not having much money in smaller notes, I gave him 10,000 Dong, about forty-three cents in US money. He said, "No! No! That won't even buy me cigarettes!" I gave him an additional couple of U.S. dollars, almost 67,000 Dong, and he seemed happy.

CHAPTER 7

Saigon—November 7, 2019

Once again joined the lobby after breakfast and met our guide and interpreter there. A younger guy, about forty-five, came up and said, "I assume you are the Bain tour group? My name is Giang *[pronounced Yang]*. I'll be your guide and interpreter for most of your trip here in Vietnam."

We introduced ourselves. Giang was Vietnamese but looked more American. He spoke perfect English, and we found he had a great sense of humor and was willing to share Vietnamese history with us, which made our experience in the country much more enjoyable and educational.

Giang said, "Elyssa from Audley tour agency gave our tour company a list of sites and things you hope to see while you're here." We nodded and smiled. Giang then looked at me. "Stan, we're still working on the orphanage, so far, we're not having much luck, but I do have some ideas." He smiled and continued, "we can talk about those later, though."

"Today, our tour covers several areas in Saigon. We have several stops scheduled, and it will be a long day. Our first stop will be a weapons cache where the VC prepared for their attack on the US Embassy. Stan, you were here during Tet Offensive in 1968, according to my notes, so you'll know what happened then." A Toyota van drove up, and Giang moved toward it. "Here's Ky to take us on a short drive."

Author's Photo Collection
Typical Side Street in Saigon

We loaded up and drove a couple of miles. Giang said, "We will be walking down a narrow alley; there will be a few market vendors to get to the weapon cache."

Author's Photo Collection
Entry into VC Weapons Cache, Saigon

The walk through the market was enjoyable. There was not much room for motorbikes and people at the same time, but everyone seemed to manage okay. I stopped and looked down a side ally. I don't know why but my thoughts went back to September 1967. There was an alley like this one, but a lady was down crying, and a young girl was kneeling next to her. My buddy and I ran down to her. She was having a baby. We kneeled beside her and did what we could to help. A baby was born. I remember it scared the crap out of me. My thoughts were interrupted by a bike horn. I pulled myself back to reality, got out of the way, and kept walking through the market; however, my mind was not on the market. I remember my VA counselor said my trip might bring back memories, but not let those memories ruin the trip. However, this was the point of this trip—which is to revisit places and events, come to terms with them, and try to put them to rest.

We walked about a hundred feet, and Giang said, pointing, "This is the entryway to an area of a weapons cache." We were standing in from of a shop that was a car repair shop in 1967, according to the sign over the door. Giang continued, "This cache was used to store weapons to be used during the Tet Offensive to attack the American Embassy."

We walked in, and Giang said, "This is Mr. Phuc Nguyen (pronounced Win). He was a Cambodia soldier during the War when he was in his late teens and is now the museum curator. He does not speak English, so that I will translate." Phuc Nguyen was about sixty years old. He explained through our interpreter the caches took several months to build and move weapons into. This happened with small groups to not raise suspicion. He said there were seventeen soldiers who took part in the Tet Offensive attack on the U.S. Embassy and that the cache supplied them.

Mr. Nguyen said there were several killed, but nine survived; some were captured and imprisoned.

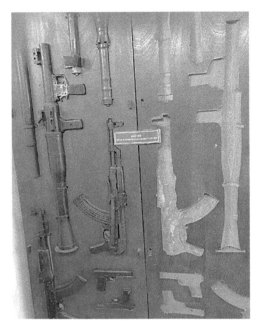

Author's Photo Collection
Two boards carved out to hide weapons to transport to the Cache

I didn't have a good impression of Mr. Nguyen, and some of the things he said I didn't believe were true, but I tried to keep in mind that they had been taught propaganda their entire life, and what they had been told was their truth.

Hearing his version of the past took me back to Đồng Tâm Base. We were hit around 0300 on the morning of January 30, 1968. I found out later from a television news story that the attack on the U.S. Embassy was instigated by a nineteen-man VC sniper team from the elite C-10 Sniper Battalion, which gathered at a VC safe house in a car repair shop at 59 Phan Thanh Gian Street to distribute weapons and conduct final preparations for the attack. Later in the news, I learned that the VC team attempted to seize the US Embassy in Saigon at the start of the VC's Tet Offensive. While the VC successfully penetrated the Embassy compound, they could not enter the chancery building and were pinned down by security forces. The lone survivor eventually surrendered to U.S. forces. Two of the snipers were later identified as U.S. Department of State employees. Their orders were to seize the embassy grounds, break into the chancery building, and take hostages. The snipers had been told by the VC Sub-Region 6 that hundreds of anti-war and anti-government university students would converge on the embassy that morning to stage a sit-down strike. The snipers also expected one or more local force battalions to relieve them at some point during the next twenty-four hours.

Author's Photo Collection
Author holding AK-47 inside the weapons cache

I'm sure there are many books written on this attack, and more details of what took place are available.

We left the museum, and Giang said, "Let's go to a little café for lunch before we go to the Presidential Palace."

The café he chose was a little one-room café full of locals, and we were the only Americans in the place. Lunch consisted of a bowl of broth, noodles, and chicken, and we each had a different drink. I chose a beer, pretty much a standard lunch.

"I remember when I was stationed in Đồng Tâm, I went to an Orphanage in Mỹ Tho," I said. "It was August of 1967, and we stopped at a Buddhist Temple on the way. On the wall by the entry was a painting of a Buddhist monk who had set himself on fire in protest of the government's treatment toward the monks. I think that was located in front of the Presidential Palace."

Giang said, "Yes, it was. However, the story that was published was wrong. What happened was the monk selected to be the victim was heavily drugged. Someone poured fuel onto the street, and the monk was picked up and set on top of it. More fuel was poured over and around him. Someone lit the fuel on the ground, and quickly spread to the monk, who died during the inferno."

That wasn't a story I liked to hear during lunch, if ever.

Once we finished lunch, our guide said, "Our next stop is a short drive to the Reunification Palace (The Presidential Palace), which was the former headquarters of the South Vietnamese Government and the residence of past presidents."

One the way, Clare asked Giang. "Did your family stay in Vietnam after the North reinvaded? How did you cope with that?"

"No," Giang said. "We lived in a small village in the Mekong Delta. When I was ten, my dad and I left to get to what we called 'The land of milk and honey... America.' We discussed it as a family, but we decided there were too many unknowns. So, my mom and brother stayed back in the hopes that once we got to America, we would be able to send for them."

"It wasn't that easy, was it? I said, " it's not like you could just jump on an airplane," I said.

"No," Giang said. "In late 1991, my dad and I took a bus to the Cambodian border, and from there, we had to sneak across the river.

The banks were muddy, and it was hard to get to the other side, but we made it across. Once there, we flagged down a motorbike taxi and were able to get to Banon District in NW Cambodia. It was about a five-hour trip on a rough and muddy road. It was the monsoon season. We finally arrived in the early evening, maybe around 7 p.m."

As we pulled into the parking lot at the Palace, Giang said, "We can talk more later. This is the Reunification Palace. It used to be the Presidential Palace during the War."

Author's Photo Collection
Palace 1967

Author's Photo Collection
Palace 2019

Several tours were going on at the time. Many Vietnamese adults and schoolchildren visited the Palace. When they saw us Americans, they went crazy, screaming "Hello!" and giving high-fives, waving, and with big smiles. I enjoyed seeing the kids; I could have hugged every one of them. I'm sure their visit to the palace was part of the training and propaganda. It was a beautiful palace; the furnishing was pretty much simple—nothing fancy like one might expect to see in a palace.

Giang said, "The Reunification Palace was the base of Vietnamese General Ngo Dinh Diem until he died in 1963," Giang said. "The Palace made its name in global history in 1975 when a tank belonging to the North Vietnamese Army crashed through its main gate, ending the Vietnam War. I think the tank is on display." We looked for it but didn't see the tank anywhere. Some areas were restricted, however, although we weren't sure why.

Author's Photo Collections
Vietnamese school children touring the Palace

The Reunification Palace consisted of five levels. Various rooms had information packets that explained the significance of each room. The basement featured tunnels, which we didn't get to, a war room, and a telecommunications center. The war command room still had the original maps on its walls displaying the locations of forces. Telecommunication equipment was also on display, defiantly dating back to the sixties. Phones are rotary dialing, communication boards with knobs to dial frequency, and toggle switches. Everything was labeled on what it was. Its adjoining basement rooms displayed war propaganda materials, with posters, books, and flags. There was a card-playing room on the third floor, while the fourth housed a casino. Reunification Palace's rooftop terrace was fitted with a heliport. It was no longer used after the War, and we did not have access to it.

After leaving the palace, we headed to the former residence of the US Ambassador of South Vietnam in the early 1960s—Mr. Henry Cabot Lodge.

The house was about a block from the heart of Saigon, in an oasis surrounded by many trees and flowers. There was the main house where the ambassador lived and a little house nearby where the Secret Service stayed. Their home had been converted into a cute little coffee shop.

Author's Photo Collection
Cabot Lodge home, living room

At the main house, we met a gentleman who was at least eighty. "Welcome," he said, extending his hand in greeting. "This used to be Ambassador Cabot Lodge's home, but now my son owns the residence and the building next door. He lives in California, but I live here to take care of the place and conduct tours. You're welcome to look through the rooms—they are marked what they are." He smiled and waited while we looked around the room.

"I like to tell you a little about the Ambassador. President Kennedy appointed him as Ambassador to Vietnam. Not sure how many people know this, but according to my history notes, Ambassador Lodge's primary goal was to overthrow the South Vietnamese Government." He opened a note book and pretty much read from his notes. He continued. "The Ambassador used his authority to organize the South Vietnamese Army resistance more effectively. Regarding Ngo Dinh Diem, the country's president, as a leader, the Ambassador felt he could not lead South Vietnam's population. Lodge worked with the generals who the United States would support a military coup against Diem's regime, which, as you know, happened in November 1963. When Lyndon Johnson became the President, he appointed Lodge to return to Vietnam in 1965 for a second tour as the American Ambassador until 1967." He stopped and asked if we needed another water bottle or soda. We said we're Ok, and he went on to read his notes, "President Johnson decided to escalate the U.S. involvement in the Vietnam War, which Lodge supported. President Johnson believed a communist takeover in the South would be disastrous for U.S. foreign policy goals."

I looked at some pictures, wondering how much of that information was correct. I was not up on my history regarding the Ambassador, but I did remember the coup—just not the date. The house was nice and was kept like it was when the Ambassador lived there.

We were shown into another room and were offered again additional soft drinks or water to drink. He continued, reading from his notes, "Mr. Lodge remained with the State Department for another ten years after leaving Vietnam; retiring in 1975, Lodge returned to his home in Beverly, Massachusetts, where he wrote his memoirs. The Ambassador died in 1985 at the age of eighty-three." He then led us through the remainder of the residence.

After leaving the Lodge residence, we drove to the war remnant's museum, which was called American Crimes Museum.

Author's Photo Collection
Barb wire cages held prisoners

The building was pretty large, and at the front door, to the immediate left, was a framed photo of Jane Fonda. My stomach turned, and my lip curled involuntarily when I saw it, but I said nothing. There were also photos of John Kerry with anti-war sentiments printed on them, along with pictures of other American politicians.

Several floors in the museum showed different aspects of the War. Many things were propaganda misleading the Vietnamese people. There were pictures of American soldier remains being dragged down a road by VC's truck, photographs showing the aftermath of battles, basically Communist propaganda, and several photos of Agent Orange, Napalm, and other terrible things. Some images were disturbing to me as some descriptions of the pictures were misleading and propaganda to sell the Communist point of view. However, nothing was said about the *good* things the allies did to help the people in the South during the War. I didn't really expect to see all truth as we knew it; I had hoped to see some good things represented. While I found the pictures interesting, I didn't spend much time in most parts of the museum.

Author's Photo Collection
Guillotine used until the 1960's

Several military equipment displays were left outside the museum building when the United States and the allies left Vietnam. This included aircraft and ground support equipment like tanks and trucks. Also displayed were cages used for captured prisoners who were unfortunate enough to be locked in, which didn't surprise me, but the guillotine did. According to the information available, the guillotine was brought by the French to Vietnam in the early twentieth century and kept for use in the big jail near Saigon. During the U.S. war against Vietnam, the guillotine was transported to the provinces in the South to decapitate the Vietnam patriots, or so the sign said. The last execution by guillotine supposedly took place in the 1960s.

The museum was busy. Most visitors were young Vietnamese, Japanese, and a few Europeans. The museum had shops and restaurants—lots of places to spend money. We spent a couple of hours there. I felt somewhat disappointed, maybe sad that the museum was so biased. Of all the places we visited during this tour, this was the only place I felt unwelcome. But I understood this is still a communist country.

We met up with Giang at the museum's restaurant. "Well, what did you think?" He asked, "I know some of the things may have been disturbing to you, Stan, but remember, this is just another way the government keeps the people in line."

I understood what he meant. "I did enjoy parts and understand what you are saying. It definitely had a bias, but I suppose that's to be expected. It was interesting."

We headed back toward our hotel. Giang said something to the driver. Giang said, "I have Ky to stop at another hotel. The Rex Hotel is a familiar landmark for Americans during the Vietnam War."

We arrived at the Rex Hotel—another nice place; we found the elevator and went to the top floor, where there was a bar. We sat down and ordered a drink. The rooftop bar looked out toward large buildings and high-rises. Giang pointed to something in the distance. "If you look toward those buildings over there," he said. "you'll see a shorter building just in front of those high-rises. That is the former CIA building where helicopters evacuated people in 1975. There were eleven trips to help people get out of Saigon before the Communists overran it. You may have seen the picture before. I think it was in *Life* Magazine."

It was hard to see, but you could see the roof top that was used during the evacuation. The building looked like it was falling apart;

it definitely needed repairs. Many new buildings and high-rises built around the area make it hard to see the rooftop of the former CIA building, but it was definitely an exciting piece of history.

Author's Photo Collection
Roof top used in 1975 for evacuation

"You may remember that on January 27, 1973, an agreement to end the War was signed," Giang said. "Two documents were signed, one between the United States and North Vietnam Government. However, due to the unwillingness of the South Vietnam Government to recognize the VC, a separate document was given to the South Vietnam Government with no reference to the VC government." Giang paused to collect his thoughts. "I believe this agreement was only to get the United States out of Vietnam." Long pause, Giang looked frustrated, "On March 29, 1973," he continued, "the last U.S. combat troops left South Vietnam; Hanoi freed the remaining American prisoners who were held in the North. America's end to what had been referred to as the 10,000-day War had ended. However, I think about 7,000 US civilian employees remained to aid South Vietnam in an ongoing war with the communist."

"Giang," I said, "did the Vietnamese think of the War as a War and not a conflict as it was referred to in the United States?"

"No people here think of it as a War, as it has been, just a different country continued on with the same War," Giang said.

We ordered another drink and looked over the view of the city. Giang continued. "Then, two years later, on April 30, 1975, the South Vietnam Government surrendered to the North Vietnamese after a major attack when the North overran Saigon, and a tank crashed through the gate at the Presidential Palace, despite the previous U.S. promises to provide air support in such a scenario, but the United States did nothing. President Nixon resigned, and now his successor President Ford could not convince your Congress to keep promises to rescue Saigon from a North takeover. Days before the fall of Saigon, evacuation by helicopter from the top of the CIA building was underway."

"I remember some of that," I said. "Just before the fall of Saigon, a project, Operation Babylift, was underway. I was interested in looking into maybe adoption at that time, so I was following this project from whatever news or information I could get. I was glued to the TV, wondering what had happened to the many trapped orphans whose future was unknown. Then I think it was in early April 1975 that Operation "Baby Lift" ended after flying almost 3,000 South Vietnamese orphans to the United States. However, the sad part was when the operation began, an Air Force Cargo jet crashed shortly after take-off from Tan Son Nhut airbase in Saigon. Most of those on board—infants and children, primarily—died in that crash. The first flight was a tragedy; however, the remaining flights took place without incident. This operation was completed two to three weeks just before the fall of Saigon."

"That was another hard time for the country," Giang said. "I understood the need to save the orphans, but it was hard on our people." He paused several minutes before continuing. "But it's true that most, if not all, would have been killed by the North Vietnamese

Army (NVA) in the end. Just because American and Australian soldiers fathered them, anything that reminded them of their presence was mostly destroyed. I don't think that was really made public," Giang said.

I sat back, remembering the orphanage and my kids and what happened at the Orphanage in Mỹ Tho in 1967, and, once back at the hotel, I didn't sleep much that night, still carrying the blame for what happened. Even after almost fifty years, it feels like it was yesterday when they died.

CHAPTER 8

Ho Chi Minh City—November 8, 2019

Today's trip was a long drive, so we left the hotel early in the morning. "We will be going to a town called Tay Ninh today," Giang said. "We will be visiting Cao Dai Temple."

We sat back, watching the countryside pass by. After the scenery and our musings had lulled us, Clare spoke up. "Giang," she said. "Yesterday, you said you and your dad made it to Cambodia. Did you stay there long?"

"No," Giang said. "We spent one night at Banon. The next morning, we had a breakfast of salty fish noodles, which they called stinky soup. It was called that because it not only stunk, but it didn't taste good either! Later that day, we found out that a boat to Thailand was available, so we took advantage of that. But when we got close to land, we were dropped off in the water several hundred yards from the shore and had to swim the rest of the way. This was around 2:00 in the morning. Once we reached the shore, we walked until we arrived at a village around 6 a.m. At one point, we saw the Tai Military Police and were happy to see them because we were told they would help us, but that wasn't the case. Instead, they checked to see if we had any money; they found my dad had a dental gold filling, pried it out of his mouth, and kept it. Later they gave us something disgusting to eat and took us to a temporary refugee camp. We were there for one month. The place we stayed in had a dirt floor and was always wet. We couldn't sleep lying down, so we tried to sleep standing up. Later I collected wood and built a bed for my dad so he didn't have to sleep on the floor."

Author's Photo Collection
Cao Dai Temple, noon service.

Giang looked out the window and noted our surroundings. "We're coming up on the Cao Dai Temple. This beautiful building is a spiritual home to an unusual blend of Christianity and Buddhism. Since it's about midday, we're just in time for worship." He parked the car, and we stepped out and stretched our legs. "We can attend from a viewing area as you walk in. The women sit on the left, and the men on the right, although I can't tell you why."

It was a beautiful temple, and we found the experience interesting. As with all the Temples we visited, the Cao Dai was beautifully done—the art, paintings, and architectural design was breathtaking.

Walking back from the temple, a young man sitting on a bench by the road got up and hurried over to Greg. He measured his height against Greg's and smiled. He thought Greg was a giant compared to him.

While in Tay Ninh City, we had lunch; our guide took us to one of the local restaurants. The lunch seemed the same as always, but I still wasn't feeling good, and everything tasted like fish, even the chicken I had. Lots of noodles were served in a bowl with broth. Not sure about the others, but I was getting tired of noodles, broth, fish, and yuk.

Author's Photo Collection
Vietnamese man thought Greg was a giant

During lunch, we got to talking about Ho Chi Minh. To my surprise, Giang said, "Did you know there were two Ho Chi Minh?"

"No, really?" I said. We were surprised. Even while I was in Vietnam in the sixties, I never heard that.

"Most Vietnamese know that Ho Chi Minh is considered singular even though there were two. The first one was educated, and as a young man, he traveled to the United States and worked as a chef in New York. He also traveled to Africa and Europe. He was an active revolutionary in the early 1930s, arrested by the Chinese and imprisoned. It was there that he became ill and died in 1936 or 38. I'm not sure about the date—it could have been much later. The imposter was Chinese, and in 1941 or 1942, he organized the Viet Minh, a communist organization. During World War II, the Viet Minh and Ho helped the Americans to rescue downed pilots. Later, Ho asked your president to help them against the French at that time. That, you know, never happened."

"I remember reading about that in one of my books on the history of Vietnam," I said. "I always wondered what would have happened if the United States had helped Ho back then. The outcome of the War would have been different. But the French were allies."

"That would have been interesting," Giang said. "Nonetheless, in 1945, when the war was over, Viet Minh took over and created the Democratic Republic of Vietnam with Ho as the president. Shortly after, war broke out with the French, which lasted about eight years until the battle of Dien Bien Phu in 1954. That resulted in the division of Vietnam into North and South. Then, in 1969, President Ho Chi Minh died of a heart attack in Hanoi."

"That's interesting," Greg said. "I never knew there were two Ho Chi Minh," Clare and I nodded in agreement.

"There's more to that story," Giang said, "but that's the general overview."

We finished our mixture of vegetables and noodles. Giang then told us about our next stop, which was the Cu Chi tunnels.

"To get there," Giang said, "we'll drive through a rubber tree plantation. At the Cu Chi tunnels, there will be a presentation by Huynh Van Chia, a VC Captain." Later I found out he wasn't really a Captain, but Giang thought he was. "Before his presentation," Giang continued, "there will be a movie explaining the purpose of the tunnels, and afterward, you will have the opportunity to ask him questions. Another guide will take us through the tunnels to explain the various rooms."

Giang phased. "The Cu Chi tunnels location was picked over the other tour location of the tunnels due to the tourist crowd. The Cu Chi location we're visiting is the least visited and will give us more time and access to the tunnels without the crowd. It will take about an hour to get there."

Clare said, "Ok, while we're traveling, tell us what happened after you and your father were taken to the temporary refugee camp?"

Giang inhaled deeply and then continued his story. "We were sent to two other camps. One was called Panat Nikchom Camp, and the other was Sikiew Camp. They were not much different from the other camps," he said. "The last camp was split into two groups based on the time they arrived. One day, someone gave me $20. Not sure why, but several knew I wanted to buy a radio. I did buy a cassette player that also had a radio. I listened to the Voice of America (VOA) and learned how to speak English. There was a British station, but I preferred the American station. I didn't want to have a British accent. We met with UN representatives who gave us a chicken to eat and thought we were in paradise."

We approached a gate, and Giang slowed. "This is the gate to the tunnel. I'll pay the entry fee and meet you over there by the trail."

We exited the car and walked into a meeting room for our group only. The speaker was Mr. Huynh Van Chia, and he started with a short movie, mostly propaganda supporting the VC effort. After the movie, our guide joined him, translating Mr. Huynh's story. Giang translated, "Mr. Huynh had lived twelve years in the tunnels, where he met his wife and had two kids. His kids were born in the caves. He now has several grandchildren." Giang paused while Mr. Huynh said more. Then Giang said, "he had lost his right arm and eye during a battle in 1968. The tunnels began during the French occupation in the late 1940s and were built over twenty-five years. The tunnels were hand-carved and expanded during the 1960s. The tunnels were a response of a poorly equipped peasant army to challenge its enemies, which had helicopters, bombers, artillery, high-tech equipment, and chemical weapons. The approximately 155-mile trail had room for caches that stored weapons and food. Rooms, a hospital, and living quarters are all connected through tunnels containing air vents, booby traps, and escape routes. This network allowed the VC to communicate between villages and evade the area's army sweeps. It allowed the VC to attack and then disappear. The material removed during construction was dumped into bomb craters, canals, and rivers. Some areas were built with various levels. Usually, the top level contained the hospitals and caches, while the lower levels were living quarters."

Author's Photo Collection
VC Soldier, Huynh Van Chia and Author

Giang paused, and Mr. Huynh said something. Giang said, "Huynh asked if we had any questions."

"Yes," I asked, "what did they do when their tunnel entries were found and they were flooded or gassed?"

Through our interpreter, Mr. Huynh said, "We would drop down to the next level. The entry locations were designed to close off easily and quickly. Each level had air vents and a drained system for water to be routed, so we were protected."

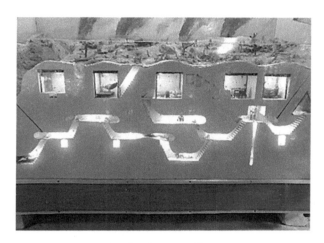

Author's Photo Collection
A display showing layout of tunnels and rooms

"I know the NVA were organized," I said, "like most armies, battalions, companies, etc., soldiers had various ranks. How was the VC organized, and what rank was he?"

Mr. Huynh said, "We were organized similarly, with regiments and divisions. Our operational levels were platoons and squads, but they were subordinate to the party organization at the village or hamlet levels that we were assigned to. They got their direction from the North. Basically, the concept of integrating political and military efforts into one objective of the North goal. In regards to rank, as soldiers, we didn't have ranks. We had what were called leaders, assistance leaders, helpers, etc. We did have some NVA soldiers as trainers."

"What about weapon supply?" I asked. "I know many of the weapons came from the North, but early on, that wasn't the case, at least. That's what I understood from our training before coming to Vietnam."

"Yes, at first, our weapons were crude by your definition. They were mostly punji sticks, spears, crossbows, and whatever we could scrounge from downed aircraft, brass, and other materials we could find to build weapons. Our weapons years later were AK-47 and machine guns, which had a similar caliber, eliminating the problem of having to supply different weapons. These came from other counties via the North," Mr. Huynh said.

"As you stated in your presentation," I said, "you lost your arm and eye during a battle. Was it the same battle?

"Yes," he said. "It was from a tank attack."

There were a few more questions, and then we left the meeting area. We followed another guide down the trails that took us past the various air vents to the tunnels.

Mr. Giang said, "Stan, I have listened to Mr. Huynh talk several times. In one of his talks to several Vietnam Vets, he said that we were all soldiers doing our jobs back then. We fought each other then, but now the war is over. I feel we are friends now, and we all need to move on with our lives."

"You think he said that to help Vets to move on and not dwell on the past?" I said.

"I think so," Giang said.

We continued with the tour going into the various rooms via small tunnels, maybe two-to-three-feet wide and three-to-four-feet high, but the rooms were plenty big to stand up and walk around.

It had to be like living in hell being in these areas during the bombing, although thousands of the enemy moved back and forth and survived. I do not thank our bombing did much to slow it down.

Most areas were marked what they were, with other information translated from the Vietnamese guide by Giang.

Author's Photo Collection
Typical punji stick traps, this one used metal punji

The rooms were set up to demonstrate real situations, a medical facility, kitchen, and workshop where various weapons and bombs were made. The tunnels were carved out; there must have been pretty stable soil as I didn't see anything shored up as you would see in a mine. There was an exhibit of booby traps with punji sticks or metal rods. The traps were wicked, one where the rods were slanted down so when your leg got trapped, you couldn't pull it out without inserting the rods deep in your leg or body, depending on the size of the trap... Ouch! I get a cold chill thinking about that! The purpose of these traps was not to kill but to maim and injure the soldier who required one or two other soldiers to help the wounded taking them out of the fight. In the process, the others frequently got tangled in those traps.

"There were tunnel rats," Giang said and smiled. "No, it's not a four-legged animal. They were American, Australian, and New Zealand soldiers trained to do a search and destroy mission inside the tunnels."

My view was this was not a promising career to be in. I understood from talking to other soldiers their casualty rate was about 33 percent or higher.

"Regarding the tunnels," I asked Giang, "I understand the Ho Chi Min Trail has many tunnels. Were they set up the same way as what we just saw?

"The Ho Chi Min Trail wasn't just one trail," Giang said. "It was an elaborate system of old paths and trails in the beginning to roads that would support larger trucks to move supplies and troops from the North and infiltrate South Vietnam. In some areas, several so-called trails were running parallel and may have been fifty to seventy miles wide, containing many routes. Mostly due to the bombing, roads were rebuilt about as fast as they were destroyed. Several teams were stationed for fast response to repair damaged roads and trails. That was one of the reasons it was so hard to stop the flow of supplies." Giang sipped some water and wiped his mouth. "This system was implemented in 1959 and continued to be widened, with more routes added, into the mid-1960s. In the beginning, it would take one month's march to travel from the North to various locations in the South. By the mid-1960s, we had underground support facilities such as hospitals, fuel-storage tanks, weapons, supply caches, and living quarters. They were very much like what we had just visited. The trail was the major supply route for the North Vietnamese forces that successfully invaded and overran South Vietnam in 1975, ending the War between North and South Vietnam."

We hit the road again. It was a long drive back to Saigon. "What happened when you met with the UN?" Clare asked Giang. "Did being a refugee get better?"

"I think the UN ran the camps," Giang replied, "but the Thai police and government forced other young boys and me to cut Eucalyptus trees that would be used for housing. These trees were in swamps filled with leeches. When we got out of the water, our legs would be covered with hundreds of leeches. The Thai police gave us limestone to scrape the leeches off. We also had buffaloes to drag the trees. They also had leeches all over them, and the leeches were boiled and fed to us.

"We spent about two years in the camps close to Bangkok in the province of Chonburi. When the rumor got out that the UN was going to send the people in the camp home, there was a revolt. People broke open the gates, and some of them were shot.

"Later, my dad and I were moved to another camp deeper into the jungle. We spent about two more years at this camp. This was the worst of them; it was more like a prison. It was a twelve-hour bus ride to get there from our last camp. About 10,000 people were in the first camp, and about 4,000 moved to the second camp. About 2,000 of those were screened off into a separate section, classified as economic refugees, and sent home." We were getting close to the hotel. Giang said something to Ky about a different route. Then he continued, "this time, there were no problems, I think most of them were ready to go home." Giang pointed and said, "Well, it looks like we're back at the hotel. I hope you enjoyed the day. Again, we covered a lot of information."

"Yes," Clare said, "we also enjoy hearing about your life; see you tomorrow."

It was a long day getting back to Saigon. "Well, I'm going to go change and head to the pool for a dip," I said.

Both Greg and Clare said they'd be there shortly.

I walked into the pool area and went to a lounge chair, and this cute Vietnamese girl came over and said, "Sir, you like your gin and tonic, double?"

"Yes, and thank you for remembering," I said. She smiled and returned shortly with my drink. I took a couple of sips before going to the pool.

Walking into the pool, as always, was cool and refreshing. I don't think the hotel knew what a heated pool was. However, it was clearly not a muddy pond like the swimming pool that was built at

Đồng Tâm base in 1967. The swim was relaxing. Both Greg and Clare joined me.

Later we walked toward the Hyatt across the street for drinks and a snack. On the way there, we talked about Giang's experience looking for freedom and how much we enjoyed his history. We walked into Hyatt to the bar. It was a nice bar and had a huge chandelier overhead. A beautiful Filipino lady was mainly singing American songs. She had a great voice; the songs were soothing and relaxing. However, I do not remember what she was singing. Busy looking at her.

CHAPTER 9

To Ben Tre—November 9, 2019

This morning came early. I was awake most of the night thinking about our trip today to Mỹ Tho and the orphanage. My thoughts were mixed with good and bad memories—what if some things were different? Well, it has been more than fifty years, so many things would be different. But my thoughts were thinking more toward the orphanage in 1967. Suppose I had never gone to the orphanage in the first place. I never got acquainted with the kids. The VC may not have gone there then, and the kids would not have died. The VC tried to destroy anything the allies were involved in. Or, only if we got there a couple of hours earlier, before the attack, we could have provided security until the Army of the Republic of Vietnam (ARVN) troops arrived, and it would have turned out differently. We could have stopped the VC, and the kids still would be alive. I still blamed myself for their death; it was my fault that the kids were no longer with us. My memories of that still haunt me every day.

I took a shower and boiled water for a cup of tea but took a shot of bourbon from a mini bottle; I got dressed and went down to the restaurant for a light breakfast. I had cereal with mixed fruit, a pastry, and a cup of tea and went back to the room to pack up and then back to the lobby to meet up with the group. Everyone was there.

"Good morning," I said.

"Good morning," Giang replied. "Today, we leave Saigon and head toward Mỹ Tho. We will stay in Ben Tre, a town across the river from Mỹ Tho."

"I remember Ben Tre City," I said. "We drove through it a couple of times during the war. As I recall, it was the main destination in the Mekong River Delta."

"Yes," Giang said. "It's now linked by paved highway and ferry boat to Ho Chi Minh City to the northeast. The area is also served by a commercial airfield and is the link to Mỹ Tho, which is still a hub in the area. We'll be there early, so before checking into your accommodations, we'll head to Stan's old base, Đồng Tâm."

Hearing the familiar names caused a mix of anticipation and apprehension. Clare seemed to sense my unease. "How long were you stationed there, Stan?"

"I was stationed for most of my tour in Vietnam," I said. "I arrived late July in '67 and left early in February '68, just before I went on R&R (rest and recuperation) to Hawaii."

"I don't know much about Đồng Tâm," Giang said, "or why the location was selected for a base."

"Before I left Vung Tàu to be assigned to Đồng Tâm, I asked several people if they knew anything about Đồng Tâm. Most only knew that they sustained frequent hits. I *found out that the MACV (Military Assistance Command Vietnam) didn't want to take land that was important to the locals and* didn't want to be based with the ARVN troops. So, the command gave the Army engineers the task of finding space suitable to construct a base in the Delta. The engineers found a location just west of Mỹ Tho, but most of that space was under water for parts of the year, so a dredging project began in late summer 1966."

"Wasn't the new base named Đồng Tâm by General Westmoreland?" Giang asked.

"Yes," I said. "The translation from Vietnamese supposedly meant *Unite Hearts and Minds*. That was the thing then—trying to win over the Vietnamese to reflect the cooperation between the United States and the Republic of Vietnam. At least, that's what we were told."

"That dredging project moved approximately nine million cubic yards, I think it was, and of mostly sand," I said, "and created nearly a square mile of land raised approximately five to ten feet to prevent flooding during the rainy season. It was like a giant sandbox. Even then, we still flooded some. When I arrived at the base, the dredging was still going on, and it was not yet finished when I left eight months later. But I think by then, it was more maintenance than building more area. The base provided headquarters for an Infantry Division, providing the US Navy a repair facility for river craft vital to maintaining regional security through the river channels.

Đồng Tâm had a short airstrip to handle small aircraft. A number of helicopters were based there as well. We had a hospital, a Signal Company, a Corp of Engineers, and a small Special Forces detachment. There may have been others also?"

"Boy, how did you dig up all that information?" Giang said.

"We were lucky to have a warrant officer who took the time to inform us where we'd be going and gave us some background information. He was great at letting us know where we were heading and what to expect. I think he was a teacher before the War and one well-respected officer."

The trip through Mỹ Tho to Đồng Tâm was not familiar at all—there had been so many changes. In 1967, the road from Mỹ Tho to Đồng Tâm was a short drive but was covered with jungle vegetation, maybe the occasional shack. Today's trip showed businesses and other buildings were within a few hundred feet from the gate into the base, although the main entrance could have been moved closer to Mỹ Tho than it was in the sixties—I couldn't tell for sure—and, of course, the entry to the base was different. We stopped about

500 feet from the gate. Giang got out and walked to the entrance of the base. Two guards walked out to meet him. One looked like an officer, and the other a soldier. After about five minutes, our guide came back.

Author's Photo Collection
Dong Tam entry 2019 Original gate was
much taller with guard towers

"Well, Stan," he began, "they said no. Our van was too big, but the main reason was they could not let any foreigners in the base without approval from the base commander. He wasn't on base, and the guard said it doesn't happen anyway if he was available."

"I didn't have much hope I would be able to enter the base," I said. "It was a long shot." I had wished I had gone with Giang to the gate. Maybe I have been able to ask the guards a couple of questions.

Giang told our driver, Mr. Ky, that we couldn't get in, and Ky said something in Vietnamese.

"Ky said he knew another way over where the Navy had its assault force during the War, and now it's a commercial port for smaller ships. Maybe a few gunboats from the Vietnamese Navy. So, he will head that way and see what happens."

Oh, shit, I thought. *I hope they have a comfortable jail ceil...*

Author's Photo Collection
Author pointing towards where the Navy River
Assault Force was located, the barracks beyond

We drove through town and back alleys and came out looking at the lake next to the base. It wasn't really a lake, but more like the backwash on a river. He pulled over by a pier, and we got out. There were some workers there. Giang went over to talk to them but returned after a brief conversation. "I asked if any of them remembered anything about the base being an American base. None of them knew anything about an American base and were surprised to hear that."

I was surprised to hear that, too, because one of them had to be in his late sixties. Then, too, he may not have lived here during that time.

We walked over to the edge of the lake. There were several small craft in the water, and across the lake, I could see several small Vietnamese Navy ships dry-docked on shore.

Giang walked over and said, "The guys here said that's the base over there. Unfortunately, that gate is closed, too, so no luck there."

"That's okay," I said. "It was a long shot." I pointed across the lake toward the boats. "See where those Vietnamese Navy boats are located?" I asked. "To the left is where the base was. You can't see the barracks because of the vegetation, but that's approximately where the water-purifying barge supplied our drinking water. The bath house was next door."

"Over that way," I said, pointing farther to the left, "was where I stayed across the road, about 500–600 feet." I paused for a moment, picturing how different it had looked in the 1960s. "The U.S. Navy had what was called the Riverine Assault Force. I remember one day, I was watching from the barracks. I was on the second floor so that I could see the Navy boats. It was October of 1967, and I saw a small boat pulling a water skier. It was right here in this lake in the middle of a war. It was wild. And over that way, farther to our left, was the airstrip."

"I remember being here in Đồng Tâm on January 30, 1968. It was about 3 a.m. on January 30, 1968. We were attacked by VC forces that were simultaneously attacking dozens of cities and military U.S. and ARVN targets throughout South Vietnam." I said.

"At Đồng Tâm, it was mostly three–four-day harassment with mortar attacks. On our worse day, there were several places that were tested with ground troops. I understood later this attempt by the VC was dealt with quickly."

"The coordinated attack by NVA and VC succeeded in achieving surprise; however, their forces were spread too thin and suffered major losses. I understood from reports that the VC as a fighting force was basically wiped out. Despite the heavy casualty toll, and its failure to inspire widespread rebellion among the South Vietnamese, the Tet Offensive proved to be a strategic success for the North Vietnamese. Tet Offensive increased negative support by the Americans back home with the demonstration, which I believed forced the end of the War, at least for the United States."

I paused for a minute, getting my thoughts together, "After getting to Vietnam, I learned that Tet Offensive is the most important holiday for Vietnamese and is a celebration of the lunar new year. In previous years, during the War, the holiday had been the occasion for an informal truce between South Vietnam and North Vietnam, including the VC."

"The Tet Offensive was planned months before the celebration to move supplies and troops in preparation for this attack. The surprise attack to hit over 120 sites aimed at creating the collapse of the ARVN and rebellion among the South Vietnamese population. The North believed this attack would convince folks back home to give up defending the South. If you could believe the news stories back home, that's exactly what happened."

We were walking back to the van, and I continued, "I remembered back to the day in 1968, I was going on guard duty, and my friend who worked in the commo center stopped me and said he had seen intel that several thousand VCs surrounded us. I made a crack about whether I should take extra bandoleers of ammo. I don't remember, but I think my friend didn't have a positive comment. I think he was frightened, at least worried. I also think the intel was such that most high-ranking officers didn't believe the information. However, we did have some damage. Our hospital was made of inflatable pods to resemble a series of halls and rooms. The air inside gave it shape, but it looked like a flat octopus when mortars hit it. I'm not sure what happened to the people inside. I didn't hear about any casualties."

We got to our van and loaded up. It was time to check into our Mekong Home Resort's accommodation. Getting to the resort was an experience. Traveling down a narrow road, making sharp turns, parts were paved and parts on graveled roads. It seemed like we were in the middle of nowhere. The road in places was so narrow that if two vehicles met each other, there would be an accident, but they seemed to get by each other at the last second. All you could do was hang on and say amen when they passed. I was glad we took out the extra insurance but hoped we never had to use it. But we made it to our stop at the Mekong Home. Actually, the stop was by their sign. The resort really was a way yet down a trail. The resort seamlessly blended into the surrounding vegetation and hamlet of Phuoc Long Village. Giang made a call, and a few minutes later, a motorbike came to welcome us, but the person pushing a cart did the work. Our bags were loaded on the cart, and we walked down a path going by several new homes being built. There were a couple of old shacks—single-family dwellings that appeared to need work—and a lot of garbage lying around. The place definitely could use some cleanup.

Author's Photo Collection
Mekong Home, open dining room.

We entered the gate at the Mekong Home into an open-air dining space. We met some of the staff, and we received our assigned bungalow. The resort was a small, maybe family-run facility. It had ten air-conditioned bungalows, and the place was formed around what was referred to as a tropical water garden and coconut trees. The resort was nicely laid out and rustic. You felt like you were part of the jungle around you. It wasn't like our other accommodation, with no swimming pools or bar; it was more like a village experience. The bungalows were more like what we would call a duplex with paths and small canals. It was a two-room, bathroom, and bedroom/living room style. It appeared to have a carpet under the bed, but it turned out to be painted to appear as a carpet; it had a mosquito net, which I didn't use. The bed was comfortable, but the pillowcases didn't smell freshly laundered. There was a small patio with a hammock; however, we never had time to try them out. One thing we were warned about was that it takes a while to get hot water. I think the hot water tank was in Hanoi because I never did get hot water. But after a long day of sightseeing, even a cool shower was refreshing. Noticing the second day at the resort, I got up at night to use the bathroom and discovered that a couple of geckos had adopted me. When I turned on the light, they took off running across the wall and hid behind the A/C. I couldn't help but think that maybe that was why I didn't have any mosquitoes in my room.

The service at the resort was okay, and the meals were all right, too, except it was pretty much the same thing every day. The dinner layout was typically a variety of pork, fish, beef, and chicken dishes—all in broth with vegetables and served in large bowls from which we filled our smaller, individual bowls. I had problems with some of the food, primarily due to not feeling well most of the trip. However, the bourbon and beer were drinkable! And it was enjoyable to sit around the dining room table and watch the sunset.

Giang had dinner with other guides but would come and join us after dinner in the dining room. Clare asked Giang more about his experience while he was in the camps. "I was training as a monk in the last camp," he said, "and I could live with the other monks. I got good food from the temple, so I would give my father two portions of my food to help him stay strong. I earned money by carrying water for people and shoveling out latrines. I was concerned for my dad. He had lost most of his teeth, and his health was failing, so I considered returning to Vietnam."

Giang sat back, enjoying his tea. "It was in 1994 when your President Clinton lifted the trade embargo on Vietnam. This opened the door for other opportunities with the UN to help us to go home. But it wasn't until 1996 that we were able to leave. The UN supervised our return; it took one month for us to get back home after going to the UN office and making arrangements. We were both offered $350 to use to get home. But only got $50 then. Three months later, we did receive $500. Then we were able to fly from Bangkok to Saigon, take an eight-hour bus ride, and then a ferry ride to the island where our home was. We reached home late in the day."

"What a trip," I said. "Most people don't realize the hardship War brings because they never experience it." The sun had gone down, and we decided to call it a night. We all were tired and knew tomorrow would be a big day. We all said good night and went back to our bungalows.

CHAPTER 10

Ben Tre / Mỹ Tho—November 10, 2019

The morning seemed to come early. I guess because I didn't get much sleep. I was restless and kept thinking about what we will find in Mỹ Tho. I finally got up around 4 a.m. and walked over to the dock. There was not much going on at the river, and there wasn't much light to see, although I could hear a few birds and ducks along the riverbank. After ten to fifteen minutes, I returned to my bungalow and laid back. I was apprehensive about going into Mỹ Tho where the orphanage was located. I had spent most of the night thinking about November 1967, when two kids died, which changed my life forever. After fifty years, it still weighed heavy on my mind. This whole trip—from the early planning stages until now—had been built around that horrible event that was as vivid as it had happened yesterday. However, the orphanage had yet to be located. In some ways, I prepared myself for the probability that we wouldn't find anything related to the orphanage. After fifty years, I was pretty sure there was nothing left, and the possibility of finding someone who was there at the same time I was there was highly unlikely.

I finally got up and took another cool shower, and got dressed. I was on edge, wondering if the orphanage could be located or if we could even find the site. By 7 a.m., I had given up any thoughts of sleep and dug out what was left of my two-ounce bottle of bourbon. Having a drink that early is something I don't normally do, but I made an exception this day. Afterward, I decided I would go over to the kitchen to see if they had any coffee or tea available. As I walked down the path, I could hear boat traffic through the heavy vegetation. I walked out on the small dock again and felt the bourbon beginning to take the edge off. Looking out over the river, there were a few patches of fog, but the sun was coming through. It was going to be another warm and sunny day. The boat traffic was light and so different from what I'd remembered—no military boats and no small arms fire or explosions in the background. I remembered looking out over the river so many years ago, awed by the jungle, and this beautiful country, thinking that *someday* it would become a resort area. But never in my wildest dreams did I think I would be standing here fifty years later, admiring the beauty of Vietnam and seeking to revisit the past.

I could hear noise coming from the kitchen behind me as the Vietnamese ladies brought the resort to life. I walked over, and one of the young ladies said, "Sir, would you like some coffee or tea?"

I said, "Yes, I would love some tea." I preferred coffee, but Vietnamese coffee was too strong for me. I sat down and put my head in my hands, hoping today that I would find some answer to the past, along with some peace. It's hard to explain the pain I feel when I think of two kids, two orphans that died—I still blame myself.

The young lady brought my tea, "Sir, are you Ok?" Her face registered genuine concern.

I looked up, and half smiled. "Yes, ma'am," I said, nodding. "I'm just waking up."

"Breakfast will be about thirty minutes," she said. "We're just getting it together."

"That'll be great," I said. "Thank you. I'm in no hurry."

Greg and Clare walked in a few minutes later. "Good morning!" Clare said.

"This is a big day, Stan. I hope our visit to Mỹ Tho will bring some relief to your nightmares and daily images."

"Thanks," I said, "it should be an interesting day. I still haven't gotten any info if the orphanage was ever located."

About then, Giang walked in. "Good morning, guys." Greg moved over to make room at the table, and Giang took a seat. "Well, today is going to be interesting," he said. "We have tried several times to locate the orphanage from your pictures but haven't had any luck so far. I think what we need to do is go to the Catholic church. About four orphanages are operating now; however, the Catholic church has been around since 1967. The others are too new to be of much help."

"That sounds like a good plan," I said.

"After breakfast, I'll call Ky and have him pick us up at the trailhead," Giang said.

Breakfast was OK. We went back to our bungalows, picked up our backpacks, and walked down the trail to the road. Ky was there when we arrived, so we loaded up and consulted Google for driving instructions. After driving around based on information from "Google," it said we found the Catholic church.

"This is the place," Giang said. "Does anything that looks familiar?"

"No," I said, "A lot of the buildings look new, and the streets are so different. There's nothing here that even comes close to looking like an orphanage." We all looked around, trying unsuccessfully to see things from a sixties perspective. "I guess I'm not much help," I said. I was disappointed that there weren't any landmarks I could recognize. I just had to remember, as it had been fifty years.

"Maybe if we go in and talk to someone, we'll be able to figure something out," I said.

"Just what I was thinking," Giang said. "We'll unload here, and Ky will find a parking place. It looks like this is the only gate open. Let's go over to the guard shack."

We walked over only to find the guard sound asleep. Giang said, "Let's walk toward the back and see if we can find someone else." We walked around and found one of the priests. He was a young guy, maybe mid-twenties and shorter. Giang spoke to him in Vietnamese.

"He doesn't know anything, but he would go and find the head Priest," Giang said.

We waited a few minutes, and the young Priest returned and spoke to Giang. "The head Priest was in a meeting, and he has asked for us to come back after lunch-maybe mid-afternoon."

Walking out, I studied the area. Nothing looked familiar. There appeared to be a school across the street from another church building.

Giang called Ky, and we found an excellent place for lunch. It was a vegetarian restaurant run by Buddhists. We had lots of food, and it was Ok. Just as I was getting tired of broth, noodles, and vegetables, it cost $15 for the five of us, which was reasonable, but the place smelled like wet dogs.

While having lunch, I was thinking about Giang and what his trip home must have been like after the War. "Giang," I said, "when you returned home, did you find everything okay? Were your mom and brother all right?"

"I walked up and found mom working in the yard. Her back was toward us. I called out to her, but she didn't turn around. After the third time, she stood up, turned around, and looked at us. She just stood there like she was just seeing things, unaware of our presence; she stood frozen in place. I called out to Mom again and told her we were home. She kneeled in disbelief for about twenty seconds, and then my parents embraced her. My younger brother, who was thirteen by then, was playing games on his computer. I figured that's what young kids did then. I told my mom I would never leave them again. I found out later my mom was, shall we say, bothered by soldiers as she was living alone without a husband there."

We understood what he had met. "That was heartbreaking for you to know what your mom had gone through. But what you and your dad went through wasn't a walk in the park either," I said.

Giang looked down; he didn't say anything but just nodded in agreement.

We finished lunch and loaded up. It was early afternoon when we went back to the church. We entered the courtyard and found the young Priest again. He waved at us and told Giang he would be back. After what seemed like a very long time, he and the head Priest came out and spoke with Giang.

"The Priest said he was sixty and has only been here about fifteen years. He didn't know anything about an orphanage fifty years ago and that we must go next door to the convent where the nuns lived. He thought maybe someone over there would know something."

I didn't think it was looking good. As I had feared, too many years had gone by for us to find anything that was helpful.

We walked over and found a gate that was not locked. We walked in. No one was in sight. Giang said, "I'll walk toward the back and see if we can find someone."

Greg went with him. Clare and I started to follow. I looked around. *Maybe* this place was familiar, but I couldn't pull it together. I looked over and saw a nun walking toward us. She was an older person. It turned out she was an essential piece of the puzzle we were trying to solve.

I said, waving at Giang, "Giang! Here comes one of the nuns."

Giang ran over and spoke to her. He asked her if there was an orphanage near her.

"Nếu có một trẻ mồ côi gần nghe."

The nun said, "Tên tôi là chị Renee các trại trẻ mồ côi là trên đường phố."

She said something, pointed across the street, and then said something more. Giang looked at me and said. "This is Sister Renee. She said that the orphanage is across the street."

Oh my god! I thought, my heart racing. How come I didn't see it? Nothing looked like it was. "Are you sure," I asked, "Nothing there even looked remotely like I remember." I felt different, my emotions churning inside and threatening to escape.

Giang said, "I'll ask her about it," Giang said, "and see if she has any information she may have regarding the orphanage." Giang turned to Sister Renee and said the following in Vietnamese, "Sister, what can you tell me about the orphanage; is this the same, or what do you know about it?"

Giang interpreted her response, "The original one was destroyed by the North Vietnamese in 1975, as it was one of those things that the Americans were involved with, and then it was rebuilt in 1978, and it is now a school/daycare and an orphanage. So, I guess we need to go over there and see what we can find out."

We thanked Sister Renee; she didn't say anything else, so we walked across the street. Walking toward the gate, I felt strange, like I was here fifty years ago; it was different; however, this is where my life changed forever. The facility had a guarded fence. We walked over to the guard, and Giang asked if we could come to enter. The guard said we couldn't and that we couldn't even take pictures. But he would go and ask someone and be back. A few minutes later, he came back and spoke with Giang.

"He said we can't come in. This school and daycare is a government facility, and the locals pay to take care of their kids, educate them, and care for them."

I felt this was the place, even though it was different. There were swings and several areas for kids to play. It was indeed an excellent place for kids. However, none of the buildings were the same; the fence was different, the entry was in a different location, and nothing looked like it did. Still, it *felt* the same.

Before we left, Clare gave me a hug and said, "It's a good thing that this space is now a place for kids to experience joy. That's a far cry from what you had to experience—loss of children who you loved."

Author's Photo Collection
Orphanage 1967

Author's Photo Collection
Orphanage 2019

I understood what Clare said but couldn't say anything. I was too overwrought to respond, so I walked over to the fence and took a moment for myself. *Can this really be the location?*

I remembered back in August 1967. It sure didn't look like this, then. The kids would have a great time in this space, which was built to entertain children. In 1967, it was just a place to house orphans. There was no other place for them during the war. But now, fifty years later, it was utterly transformed. I thought about my two kids and could see their smiling faces. It hurt to think about them, wishing things had been different. I walked back to the others.

We thanked the guard, and Giang asked us what we wanted to do. "It's getting late," I said, "So let's go back to the Mekong Home and talk about a plan for tomorrow." I needed a nip, something more substantial than water.

Giang called Ky, and he came by and picked us up, and we headed back to the resort.

I'm sure each of us had different feelings about what we learned that day. It took a lot out of me, but I couldn't help but feel there was more we needed to find out. I knew from Clare's expression she was concerned about how the day's experiences had affected me.

We got to the Mekong Home and decided to have a drink before dinner. The resort had beer and wine, which made for a relaxing evening.

"How do you feel about today?" Greg asked.

"I don't really know," I said, "It was like we were solving a mystery and hit a cold trail. Today was kind of tough, but I can't help but feel like something is missing."

"Well, we think we need to go back tomorrow, and you should talk more with Sister Renee. Maybe she knows more, but we need to ask the right questions," Clare said.

"Yeah," I said. "You're right. We need to talk with Giang in the morning; a change in our schedule is needed." After all, the real purpose of the trip was the orphanage.

We said good night and planned on talking to Giang about the schedule for tomorrow.

That night I was restless. I had to take some pain pills to get to sleep finally, but even then, I woke up thinking about the two kids several times. If only we had been brought to the orphanage several hours earlier those many years ago, perhaps it would have been different. Who could say?

CHAPTER 11

Back to the Orphanage—
November 11, 2019

The morning started with an excellent breakfast, but I didn't eat much. "Happy Veteran's Day," Clare said, "and thank you for your service."

I hadn't realized it was November 11th. I had too many other things running around in my head and had forgotten entirely. How appropriate. I smiled and shook my head, half-smiling. "Thanks," I said.

Before we were finished with breakfast, Giang appeared. "Well," he said. "What do you want to do today?"

"We were talking last night," I said, "and thought we needed to go back to the convent and talk more with Sister Renee. We think she knows more, and maybe she can answer a few questions that might shed more light on what happened at the orphanage. There's more to Sister Renee's story. We thought if we ask the right questions—now that she's had a chance to think about it—maybe she'll open up some more."

"I will call Ky and have him pick us up and tell him that we have a different schedule for today," Giang said.

"Thanks, Giang," I said. "This is important."

Several minutes later, we were on the road back to the convent. When we arrived, we found another nun and asked to meet with Sister Renee. She took us to a meeting room, gave us water, and told us to be seated and that she would find Sister Renee. Several minutes later, Sister Renee walked into the meeting room. She seemed to be happy to see us and sat down next to me.

"Thank you, Sister, for meeting with us." Giang spoke to her in Vietnamese, "Stan has a picture and was wondering if you could recognize it."

Giang looked in my direction and nodded. "Show her the picture with the two nuns, Stan."

Author's Photo Collection
Author and Sister Renee

I showed her a picture that Audley travel sent me showing a statue with a soldier and two nuns. Audley was investigating the orphanage's location and had sent me the picture to see if I could recognize the statue in the background.

Giang interpreted, "Sister said she remembers; this is Sister Joseph on the right and Sister Emily on the left. They are both dead now, and she doesn't remember the soldier's name. But he was here a couple of years ago but looked old."

We all chuckled; I showed her a picture of me in my book and asked her if I also looked old. She just smiled, but she didn't say anything. As we talked, we found out she was seventy-four years old and retired two years ago, from what I thought. Does a nun really retire? Also, she was the last of the living nuns who were here during the War.

I finally had to ask her, "Sister," I said, "do you remember when the VC attacked the orphanage in November 1967?"

Giang translated the question for her. She thought about it and told Giang. Giang translated back, "Renee said yes; her friend died during that time."

Oh god! I thought. I looked at the others and said, "She's talking about the nun and the baby I found dead when I entered the courtyard during the attack."

I couldn't believe this. I knew I would never find anyone who was at the orphanage in 1967 and that probably the orphanage was also gone. But interacting with someone who was essential there took me back. I was afraid to ask the following question.

Author's Photo Collection
Showing Sister Renee pictures of the orphanage in 1967

75

I turned to Giang and said, "Ask Sister Renee if she remembers anything about a couple of kids dying during that time?"

Giang asked Sister Renee and then translated her answer.

Giang said, "She heard something about the VC in the area. She was a principal at the school across the street at that time and was not allowed to come out. The ARVNs arrived; it was a while before she and others could leave the building. The ARVNs had taken her friend's body, and there were a couple of kids, but there wasn't anything for them to see. She found out they had died but did not know the details."

Clare told Giang, "Interpret exactly what I tell you."

Giang nodded and said, "Yes."

Clare began to tell Sister Renee what happened to the kids. She had read the story in my first book, and we had talked about it many times in preparation for this trip. Clare knew it almost as well as I did, and she knew how it had affected me. I was glad she could tell the story while we sat there because I knew I couldn't.

I sat there, tears running down my cheeks. I couldn't help it. For more than fifty years, I have been living with that memory. It was as much a part of me as anything in my life's experience. As horrible as it was and as difficult as it was to live with, it was even harder to let it go. It will always be with me.

No one said anything for a couple of minutes. Greg said, "Sister, would you pray for Stan?"

Sister Renee nodded. She took my hand and held it tightly. She prayed silently.

When she looked up, Clare asked, "Do you have an e-mail address where we could send you a picture or a note?"

Giang asked Sister Renee about e-mail and then chuckled. "Sister Renee doesn't know what e-mail is."

We smiled. Giang asked if maybe the office would have that information, so she went to the office to see if there was an e-mail address. She returned a few minutes later with a piece of paper with the e-mail address and their website written on it.

Before leaving, we hugged each other and gave her 500,000 Dong. She didn't have a need for money but said it would help the school. About a month after I returned home, I sent her an e-mail with a picture of the four of us, but I never got any reply.

I told Giang, "I know visiting Bearcat was on the schedule for today, and I know it's out of the way. So, I'm for doing something else—or calling it a day." I was mentally wiped out but didn't want to spoil the plans.

Clare spoke up and saved the day. "How about we find a liquor store and get some whiskey."

"I'm all for that," I said. My little travel bottle had long been empty.

We drove around and found a couple of liquor stores, one with parking available. They had lots of booze but not too many we recognized. After much searching, we found what we were looking for.

Greg and I enjoyed bourbon and coke or two at the Mekong Home before dinner. Dinner was more rice and soups. I was missing a good old hamburger and fries. A hamburger that tasted like beef that is.

We were all tired and hit the rack at 8 p.m. It had been an emotional day for all of us. I lay there thinking about how lucky we had been to talk to a nun who was actually there on that awful day. The odds of that happening were extremely slim, but the fact that it did, and that she had been at the orphanage and knew the nun who was killed that fateful day, was like a gift. She helped bring some closure of a sort to an extremely troubling chapter in my life. I felt somewhat less burdened as a result of her prayer—even if I didn't understand it—and was confident I would rest a little more peacefully that night.

Giang joined us for breakfast. "Stan," he said, "I understand that the incident regarding the kids at the orphanage was a trauma for you. I am a Buddhist, and a Buddhist does not dwell in the past. This happened fifty-two years ago, Stan. I think it is time to let it go."

I understood what he was saying. "But I'm not a Buddhist," I said, "I know War is different for every veteran, and I understand Buddhist view would be different."

Giang said, "The Vietnamese did not experience PTSD."

It was an interesting observation, I thought. *I'm sure some Vietnamese soldiers also had problems dealing with the War; it wasn't easy for them either.*

After I got home, I did some research on PTSD with Buddhist Monks and VC/NVA soldiers and found that both *did* experience a form of PTSD. Buddhist monks who the Chinese tortured were suffering from PTSD. And VC/NVA soldiers who were involved with heads being cut off and put on a stick, etc., had flashbacks and felt they were haunted. So, it wasn't quite as simple as Giang made it sound, although I appreciated the sentiment and his efforts to help me to move on.

That day we toured a modern market that Giang described as "like your Walmart," and he was right! They sold clothing and food, housewares and hardware, and they even had an actual toilet!!! Clare was happy to hear about the bathroom.

A Vietnamese student came up to Greg and planted himself in front of him. He smiled nervously and said, "I'm doing a class project, and we're supposed to ask questions to foreigners. Is my question, do you have a problem with kids getting addicted to video games? And, if so, what is your solution?"

"Yes, we do," Greg said. "I try to get my kids involved in sports or other activities." The student took some notes and thanked Greg for his time.

We went upstairs to the mall, and I took a picture of a Dairy Queen (DQ). Clare did the same thing but was interrupted by a Communist security guard, who told her NO PHOTOS!

78

From there, we went into a bookstore, and I was surprised to see so many books on Trump—both for and against him—along with books by Suzie Orman and Warren Buffet. The titles were all in English, and I did not look to see if they were translated into Vietnamese. We left the bookstore and decided to try the ice cream at the DQ. It tasted as good as it did at home, and we savored every bite.

One of the young ladies who was doing the same class project as the young man was standing by the stairs. It looked like she was waiting for someone. I walked over to her and said, "Excuse me, does your school teach you anything about the Vietnam War?"

"Yes," she said, "We learn the history and know you and other veterans from America and other countries came to help the South to become a free country." She continued, "Does your country teach about the Vietnam War?"

"That's a great question," I said. "The Vietnam War was not well supported, and from what I have heard from our kids, I feel they were not told the whole story—only the negative stuff. Or maybe the teacher wasn't informed about Vietnam to be objective. At least, that's what American kids tell me when I ask. That might be a good research project for me when I get home. But my guess is you have a better understanding of the War than American boys and girls." I thanked her for her time and wished her luck with her schooling and future.

I caught up with the others, "Hey, Giang," I said, "I noticed several books in the bookstore, different views of President Trump. Do the Vietnamese like or dislike President Trump?"

"It depends," he said. "Yes, they like him when he puts tariffs on China, but they don't much care for him if he is helping China. Vietnamese dislike the Chinese, and if another country leader is doing something against China, they like him, and when they help China, they hate them."

"That is interesting," I said, "I get the Chinese connection when you think about all the fighting between Vietnam and China."

Giang nodded. "So, you want to visit another market for shopping?"

"I think we want to go by the Catholic church again to visit Sister Renee on a few other questions," Clare and Greg nodded in agreement, and so Giang called Ky to pick us up and take us back to the Catholic church.

The drive didn't take long, and once back at the Church, we parked the car and walked into the courtyard. Two nuns were walking toward us, and we asked to see Sister Renee. They said Sister Renee was not around, but we asked the two nuns if they remembered the existence of the orphanage in 1967. As they did not work there at that time, they didn't have any information regarding the orphanage.

We walked across the street again for one last look at the kindergarten. I took it all in—the children, the playground equipment, the laughter—and found some satisfaction in knowing the site of the old orphanage was now a place where young children were cared for, educated, and able to play without fear. We left the orphanage for the last time and returned to the Mekong Home. It was a quiet drive, and I was lost in thought and tired.

In an effort to stay awake, I asked Ky, our driver, "What do you do when you drop us off for several hours before you pick us up again? Must be boring?"

"Oh no!" he said, "I go fishing."

"Fishing!" I said. "What do you do with the fish."

"Well, nothing," Ky said, "I don't catch any worth keeping." We all laughed.

Before arriving at the Mekong House, we stopped at an ATM and drew another one million dong (about $43). Once back at the Mekong House, we had dinner. We were scheduled to embark on our cruise up the Mekong River the following day. We just sat back and enjoyed the evening. I asked Giang, "After you returned home, what did you do?"

"I went back to school," he said. "I went to college and got two degrees—both in business. I did well in school and was top of my class and even gave lectures to my fellow students. I thought one day I'd like to be an Ambassador for my country. My grandfather worked for the French when they were in control, but now that wouldn't happen— with the Communists now in control. When my brother grew up, he went to Teacher's College, but he didn't like it and didn't want to be a teacher. He enjoyed computers, so I sent him to college for three years to become a computer programmer. My brother now works as a website designer for a foreign country. I think somewhere in Europe."

"Well, I'm about to crash," I said. "It's been a long couple of days. I'll see all of you in the morning."

I walked into my bungalow, fixed myself another drink, and then walked over to the patio door and looked out over the land-scape. Thinking about the day and our visit to the orphanage took me back to November 1967—the last time I saw "my kids." The "what if" question reared its ugly little head again. What if I had been there earlier and was able to save the life of those two children, the ones I thought of as "my kids." What if I had been able to bring them home when I left Vietnam…how would my life have been different? I played the tape repeatedly in my mind, thinking I should never have gone to the orphanage in the first place. Then, maybe, I wouldn't have become so attached to them. And if I hadn't become so attached, the VC might not have sought to punish us by hurting them. And if I had not loved them enough to spare them unbearable suffering and torture, all of our lives might have been different, but would they have been better? Those were questions I wrestled with every day of my life.

CHAPTER 12

Ben Tre – Mango Cruise—
November 12, 2019

We checked out of the Mekong Home, took pictures, and said goodbyes to all the workers. A friendly group of people.

"The help here liked you guys," Giang said. "They told me it was because you all laughed all the time."

Author's Photo Collection
Author next to our Sampan cruise on Mekong River

"We enjoy life and find lots to laugh about," Clare said. They gave Clare one of their small bowls we ate out of as a souvenir.

We headed to Mango Cruise resort. It was about a one-and-half-hour drive. There we met our guide for the cruise. Giang would meet with us down the river in a couple of days.

This was a two-day, one-night trip down the Mekong river. Our sampan was almost seventy feet by about fourteen feet wide; it had two bedrooms and a full bathroom with a shower and tub. There was a dining room, a living room, and a crew's quarters; it was a small vessel for six people plus a crew.

We walked along a dock to the sampan, where our luggage was loaded. We were introduced to the crew, sat down, and had another coconut drink. I think the tour description by Audley said we would enjoy a welcome cocktail while we enjoyed the fresh air on the Mekong Delta. A fruit drink, maybe pineapple and coconut juice, the fresh air on the Mekong varied as the river was pretty muddy and polluted but didn't smell. Afterward, we were told we would be going to another place for a snack. Afterward, we would take a small traditional wooden boat that someone would paddle like a canoe down a waterway and meet up with the sampan. We were loaded on a motorbike that was converted into a small truck-like vehicle. We bounced around for several minutes, going down roads that needed work done. We weren't told that was going to happen, but we finally reached our destination and walked a short distance to a covered area. It was a nice walk after bouncing around getting here.

Waiting there for us were various fruits and other snacks. Not sure why it did not impress us. Afterward, we walked a short distance along a path to a waterway and a small dock that was about ready to fall apart. We were helped into a smaller boat; I guess that was the traditional wooden boat. It was about two feet wide and maybe fourteen feet long. The three of us, our guide, and two crew climbed in. The crew, a lady up front, was paddling the total time, and a man in the back paddled on occasion and steered the small craft. Come to think of it. It seemed like the women working and the men took the easy way out of tasks…that was pretty much true when I was here during the War. Our guide sat toward the back. He played his harmonica and sang Louis Armstrong's Swanee River and What a Wonderful World songs. I enjoyed it. Not sure if anyone else did. That's about the only time he talked, as he was not much of a guide. Sure, missed Giang. Not something that was in the plan.

After about an hour of navigating through the canal, we met up with our cruise sampan. We were helped aboard and started up the river heading to Cần Thơ. Along the route, we stopped at a brick-making facility.

Author's Photo Collection
Recycled coconut made into building bricks

This was an interesting stop. Coconut shells were recycled. The hair on the shell was cleaned off to make rope. Part of the shell was crushed and made into a mud-type material and put through an extruder forming bricks. They were stacked in piles to dry. Then they were moved to a kiln fireplace and were baked at 400 degrees for several days. Then they were set aside for several days before being used in the construction of homes, walkway, fences, and other products. The ashes were mixed with other materials to make fertilizer. Just about everything is recycled. Plastic, for example, is recycled, and plastic bottles are not allowed in most hotels. They provide glass water bottles; you can refill them from a water cooler in the hallway.

Back on the sampan, we relaxed with a drink, had our own stuff, and enjoyed the scenery. I was amazed at the number of ships using the river. Many of them were hauling gravel that was dredged out from the river bottom. Most of the gravel was used for building concrete bricks. Others had bags of rice and other farm products. During the War in 1967, most of the river traffic was military patrol boats and small sampans. I think the river then was muddy. Now the river seems to be more polluted—lots of debris and dirt. Yet the locals still swim in it and do their laundry on the banks.

After a good lunch, mostly cheese, shrimp, and fruit, we stopped for a short walk through a market, as you would find in Tijuana, Mexico. There was a lot of "stuff" to spend money on. I noticed that there were not that many people shopping. I did stop by a woodworking vendor. I bought my brother in Montana a carved Harley—he owned a Harley. The lady told me they made the wood-carved products, but I think I was being told a little story. There was a guy carving something. It looked like he had been cutting on it for some time. I think it was just for show, and I probably got the carvings from China.

Back on board the Sampan, we got ready for dinner. Dinner was advertised as a cooking demonstration. We made our own spring rolls, and then they were taken back to be cooked. However, Greg popped it in his mouth on his first spring roll. The cook told us it was not cooked yet. Oh well, we also had veggies, a noodle dish that was a little spicy, a fish dish with coconut, and then a fruit combination of pineapple, watermelon, and mango for dessert. I wonder why one of the crew stood by the exit toward our rooms. He didn't seem to pay much attention to the cooking demo but more attention to what was going on down the hallway. I thought it was unusual but didn't think much about it at that time.

We were done, and it was almost dark, so we went to our rooms which were in the center of the boat next to a narrow hallway. The room was closed off with a curtain, and the bed had a mosquito net already in place. I was tired and ready to go to sleep, but the engines hummed along. I finally dozed off. Boom, I was awakened. Apparently, the sampan was hooking up to a bowie for the night but ran into it. Oh well, if we were going to sink, someone would have said something. Come to think of it. We never had an emergency drill or life jackets. What the heck if my feet started to get wet; I'll worry about it then. I rolled over, covered my head, and went to sleep.

CHAPTER 13

Cần Thơ—November 13 and 14, 2019

Today, we were to meet Giang and Ky in Cần Thơ, which is the biggest city in the Mekong Delta; the name came from the "river of poems." The town is famous for its floating markets, Buddhist Pagodas, food and fresh fruits, and the beauty of the Mekong delta. Cần Thơ is located on the Hau tributary, the larger branch of the Mekong River on which we were on.

That morning we woke up when the sampan was on the move. I noticed the river was in full swing with floating markets and heavy ship traffic. After breakfast of scrambled eggs, toast, and various fruits and tea, we pulled over near Cần Thơ to take a short walk through nurseries. Several nurseries provided shrubs and plants for the many hotels throughout the city. It was an interesting trail along a small canal. Several of the locals were taking their morning walk or scooter ride to work.

After about an hour, we were back and loaded back up on the sampan. After about thirty minutes, we were on the other side of the Mekong River, where we tied up along a busy street in Cần Thơ. Several food markets also have businesses providing services of dental work and being fitted with glasses. These were located in small shops. Markets were open-air, providing fish, pottery, and various vegetables.

Author's Photo Collection
Visiting one of the oldest homes in Vietnam

Our walk took us to a place where we would visit one of the oldest homes in Vietnam. We walked into a courtyard where this home was located, noticing it needed repairs, and indeed a new paint job was in order. The roof was a traditional convex and concave interlocking tile known as Yin and Yang style roofing.

A pretty young lady met us at the steps, introduced herself, and led us inside. She told us about a love story of a young French girl and a wealthy Vietnamese businessman. They could not marry because she was French and poor. I think they did live there if I recall the story. The interior was mostly French architecture and beautiful wood. The existing furnishings were old, and some needed repairs. There was a dining room, bedrooms, and living rooms, but all could have used additional furnishings. The young lady said the home was open to the nightly rental, including dinner. I don't recall what they rented for or what was offered for dinner. To me, it didn't look like it was ready for customers. I didn't think I would be interested; it would be boring except for simply saying that I slept in the oldest home in Vietnam. Not something on my bucket list.

We walked back to where the sampan was located and met up with our guide Giang and driver Ky. They had our bags loaded and ready to head out to our hotel. We said goodbye to our sampan crew and gave the captain a tip to share with the crew.

We loaded up. I was offered the front seat. I sat back, relaxed, and enjoyed our drive to our hotel, Victoria Cần Thơ. Giang talked some about Cần Thơ. I don't remember much about that, as I think I dozed off. We arrived at our hotel. This was another nice hotel. We were met by the hotel staff, who served as a fruit drink. After checking in, Giang said he would be back and join us for dinner. We dropped our stuff off in our rooms, and it was time for a trip to a pool. There were two nice pools, but the water was cool; it took a minute to get in. But once in, it felt great. We swam around and then flagged down one of the pool servers. We ordered drinks and a small snack of fruit and cheese. The hotel staff pampered us and checked on us if we needed anything. We found most hotels we stayed at were well-staffed and provided good customer service.

"I was going through my purse," Clare said, "and found that some of the U.S. dollars were missing. This had to happen during breakfast or maybe during dinner on the cruise. None of the Dong was missing, but $180 of the U.S. money was missing."

"I think I was missing a couple of twenties, too," Greg said, "but though I may have spent it? However, I always used Dong, so I wasn't sure where it went."

Later, we told Giang what had happened, and he informed his travel office. "The office said they would look into it," Giang said, "but probably nothing would happen. However, his office wanted to buy us dinner that night and was sorry about the incident." I couldn't help but wonder if that happened while we were having dinner while one crew was standing watching the hallway.

We were scheduled tomorrow to do a motorbike tour around the city. I think we were toured out, and when Giang came back for dinner, we asked him to cancel the morning tour. It was time to take a break and just relax before heading to Vũng Tàu.

That evening we had a nice dinner along with Giang, listening to his story about his journey in a concentration camp in Cambodia and later in a prison camp, Vietnam re-education camp while he was returning home.

I asked Giang, "Did you and your brother get married?"

"My brother was thirty-eight," Giang said, "and he was in a relationship, but my mom was superstitious, so she got the girl's birth date and had her checked out by a fortune teller. She didn't like what she found out, so she told my brother, 'DO NOT MARRY THAT, GIRL!' So, he's single."

Giang paused for a bit sandwich. "I got married when I was thirty-five. I was a little upset with my parents because they did not attend my wedding in Saigon. I think they were mad I got married."

"When my wife Tuyen (pronounced Twin) had our first child, I called my mom to tell her that she had a grandson! When I was thirty-four, my mom kept calling me and wanting to know when I was going to get married and give her grandchildren. So, I told my mom she got her to wish complete and now had a grandchild."

I asked Giang, "When were you born?"

"Good question," he said, "I can't tell you the exact date as I don't know, and I have asked my mom, but she doesn't remember the date either."

We finished our dinner, and Giang said he'd see us in the morning. I decided to hit the pool one more time. I had a relaxing swim and went to my room and took a hot shower, a long hot shower, and hit the rack.

CHAPTER 14

Vũng Tàu—November 15, 2019

We started the day out with an excellent breakfast buffet of American and Vietnamese foods at the Victoria Hotel. Today we were to leave Cần Thơ for a six-hour drive to Vũng Tàu. Vũng Tàu was the location of my first assignment and the site of my in-country R&R. Vũng Tàu was famous for the beach, and for the locals, it was a significant vacation spot.

"Stan," Giang said. "When you were stationed in Vũng Tàu, what did you think of the place, I know it was used for in-country R&R, so it must have been pretty nice, huh?"

"I was there in 1967," I said, "just what I have seen. I knew this place would be a worldwide tourist location with significant hotels. Just a matter of time before the War was over. The base was surrounded by white sand but was not close to the beach, so I never made it there. Duty there was not what I would call routine in Vietnam. True, it was Vietnam, but it ran more like we were in the United States. Like having haircuts, getting shaved, clean light-starched fatigue, spit-shinned boots, and shining belt buckles, but we *did* have *mamasan*. This was all for about a couple of pennies a day for Vietnamese maids to keep uniforms and boots looking good. Not sure if the other units stationed at Vũng Tàu had the exact uniform requirements.

Yes, the R&R center was there, and I did get a three-day R&R later in my tour. The center was downtown near the bars and interment, not even close to the beach."

"What about duty? Giang said.

"It was different," I said. "Duty there did not feel like you were in a War zone. I did not have a weapon until I had guard duty, but I had to check it back to supply. Come to think of it. I did not have a weapon permanently assigned until I was transferred to Đồng Tâm. I'd been in the country almost six weeks by then."

"Isn't that unusually not to get a weapon when you got there?" Giang said.

"I hope it was unusual," I said. "I'm sure soldiers got a weapon soon after getting there, especially if you were assigned to a combat unit."

We were silent for a while after that. The view out the window was quite beautiful. Our route took us back to Saigon and then East to Vũng Tàu. This was a nice drive. The route took us through the countryside.

My mind wandered back to February 1968 when I was on a convoy to Saigon, maybe the same road, but now it was paved. Back then, I remember we were the last in the convoy. We kept dropping back as our Deuce and a Half didn't have the power to keep up. I remember getting to a graveled intersection, the main convoy was out of sight, and we weren't sure which way to go. We decided to take the route that appeared to have the most traffic. Several miles later, we could see the place seemed to be Saigon; we finally started breathing again. My mind wandered back to reality.

Author's Photo Collection
Highway 1 in 1967

Author's Photo Collection
Highway 1 2019

"Yeah, I guess I was. I was thinking about being in convoy to Saigon and almost getting lost. It sure is different now."

"I bet things are different for you after what you experienced," Giang said. "Some things don't change, especially for the Vietnamese farmers. Many rice farms and locals work the fields along our drive. As you can see, the rice fields are sectioned off in different stages of growth. So that they would have some fields being planted, while others are being harvested, giving a regular supply of rice."

Interesting, I thought. I guess that was the way it was back in the sixties. I sat back and relaxed, watching the scenery go by. I assumed I dozed off for several minutes. I think I was emotionally drained. The orphanage took a lot out of me.

I heard Giang say something about a city we were about to drive through; it was called Tràng Bàng. I remember that city and woke up out of my daze.

Giang said, "This city gained notoriety when a Pulitzer Prize-winning image depicted a little nine-year-old girl running down the road naked and burned on her back during a South Vietnamese napalm attack; her name was Phan Thi Kim Phuc. You may have seen the picture in Life magazine. That incident occurred on June 7, 1972, when elements of the North NVA occupied the town of Tràng Bàng."

"People back home always thought the United States was responsible for that," I said.

"I heard that," Giang said. "But I think all the US troops and allies had left Vietnam by then. The ARVN Vietnamese Air Force dropped napalm on what was thought to be the NVA stronghold. It was a three-day battle, and the ARVNs mistakenly dropped napalm on civilians—a disaster of War that happens regardless of any safeguards for such thing."

Giang paused, getting his thoughts together, "This little girl is now grown and has gone through many surgeries, many in the United States, and now I think she lives in Canada. A great book called The Girl in the Picture – The story of Kim Phuc and her friends helped her establish the Kim Foundation International. The foundation's mission is to help children who are underprivileged victims of war. She did some great things with the funds she received from the foundation."

We stared out the windows, lost in our thoughts. I remembered well the story of the little girl and the shock of seeing her running down the street with other children, her burning clothes torn off, and her face registering absolute terror. And I remembered the two kids in Mỹ Tho and the incident that ended their lives and changed my life forever. It seemed so unfair that innocent children had to suffer and die for causes they couldn't possibly understand.

The trip was coming to an end, and I was pretty much ready for it to be over. It had been fascinating to see places I had first encountered as a young man during the Vietnam War, and our visit to Mỹ Tho *had* afforded me some closure. For that, I was grateful. We had seen how beautiful the country could be—as I had anticipated fifty years before—and Clare, Greg, and I had deepened our friendship and love for one another. As the trip wound down, I felt it had accomplished its purpose and then some.

We arrived at Imperial Vũng Tàu, just across the road from the ocean. The hotel was another beautiful and comfortable place. Many areas in Vietnam have geckos, and our hotel posted a sign that said, "As we live in an environment with a vast tropical fauna, you may encounter small geckos. They eat insects, are completely harmless, and help protect people from tropical diseases. We hope you enjoy your stay at the hotel!" The geckos were not any problem. They stayed out of our way, and most of the time, we didn't even see them, although we sometimes heard them running across the walls at night.

CHAPTER 15

Vũng Tàu—November 16–17, 2019

After a good night's sleep and a breakfast of American, French, and Vietnamese foods, we enjoyed the pool the rest of the morning. Later I walked across the road toward the beach. It took me fifty-four years to finally make it to the beach in Vũng Tàu; I was surprised. The pure white sand on the base did not exist on the beach; even if it did, it appeared to be very polluted now.

The hotel was beautiful; the only negative was the night barking dog next door. Giang joined us, and we went for a walk looking for a local restaurant. We found a Venezuelan restaurant next door. It was kind of like Hooters with loud music. Giang ordered fried frog, Greg had chicken wings which he didn't like, and Clare and I had beef and vegetable skewers. We both commented that the beef didn't taste anything like American beef, and the fact that we never saw any stray dogs running around made us both suspicious. I knew Vietnamese beef came from Australia and suspected it had a different taste, but I haven't convinced our skewers were any kind of beef at all. We decided not to put too much thought into it and to simply enjoy the rest of the evening and the walk back to the hotel. Despite our attempts at positive thinking, my stomach did somersault the rest of the evening.

We walked into the hotel lobby, noticed a casino, and walked in to check it out. Several foreigners were playing with their machines. Giang was stopped at the door and was asked if he was Vietnamese. Giang said, "No, I'm American. Don't I look like an American?" They let him in.

"What was that about?" I asked.

"The government does not allow Vietnamese people in casinos. It's the Government's way of ensuring they don't lose their money and have to be supported by the Government."

I said, "not a bad idea, but it probably wouldn't work for Las Vegas."

We decided to call it a night. Greg and Clare arranged a room for Giang at the same hotel. His company required him to stay at a cheaper hotel to minimize costs, so he enjoyed the upgrade.

That night was a bad one for me. I was sick most of the night, throwing up and feeling lousy. Maybe it was the dog. By morning I was feeling better and ready for another day.

Breakfast included foods from Asia, Britain, Scandinavians, and America on this day. There were lots of Vietnamese people as guests staying at the hotel; it must have been a local holiday. Later that morning was pool time, and then we met in the bar for a drink. It was relaxing; the waitress came over, "May I help you with your favorite drink?"

"Yes, I think so," I said. We gave her our drink order, "You speak excellent English; what part of the world is your home?"

"I'm Filipino. I've been here a couple of years. I went to school in the United States for several years," she said.

Two gentlemen walked by our table, and the taller of the two stopped. "Hi, I'm Jeff," he said, offering a handshake. "I'm the hotel manager; you folks enjoying your stay?"

We said, "Yes, you like to join us?"

"Sure," the other guy said, "By the way, I'm Daryl, the General Manager."

"You're not Vietnamese," Greg said, "Is your descent English?"

"I was born in England but have lived in Canada and then Tokyo," Daryl replied. "Now, I live in Vietnam, and I've been with this hotel for about six weeks."

Jeff said, "I am from Europe but have lived in Vietnam for twenty-seven years."

They were businessmen investing in hotels and other hospitality businesses.

During our conversation, Jeff said, "If you want to learn how to do money laundering, this is the guy. He is the best."

We were taken back for a minute. "Okay," I said cautiously, stealing a look at Clare and Greg. "Is there an easy way?"

"Yes," Daryl said. "There are a couple of ways." He pulled his chair up close to the table and leaned in. "If I'm going to travel to Europe, for example, I'll buy up a couple hundred thousand in diamonds—they don't register to go through security—and then cash them in at my destination. But most times, I just do a transfer from my bank account to many other accounts in other countries."

"Now, doesn't Vietnam banks and government track that?" I said.

"Oh yeah," Daryl said. "But they only report amounts of $10,000 or more. So, you transfer $9,999 to different banks, and then you move that around until you have it where you want it."

"Well," I said. "Great, but I would need a spare $9,999 lying around to do that. And why would I need to do that, anyway?"

"Well," Jeff said, "If you had several million that had to be moved, there are easy ways to do it."

"I don't think there is any chance of that happening," I said.

Jeff said, "Maybe someday." He smiled a crooked smile.

The subject changed. Others talked, and then Jeff wanted to know more about Greg's hotel back in Montana. There was some talk about that—website, payments, etc. I didn't follow most of what they were talking about.

Daryl listened to Greg's description and nodded thoughtfully. "I could help you out with that," he said. "I can easily create you a website that sort of bypasses the OTAs."

I didn't know what OTA was and wasn't going to ask. "Well, *this* has been an interesting afternoon," I said. "But we need to get ready to go. Giang was going to take us to Kelly's bar."

"Oh yes," Jeff said. "That's a great Australian hangout."

We stood to leave. "Thanks for the information," Greg said.

"Yes, of course," Daryl said. "Maybe I'll run into you before you leave. Have a nice visit, and enjoy the rest of your trip." Then he turned to me and said, "Hope it helps you with the PTSD."

"Thank you," I said, wondering how he knew about that and the reason for our trip. We had said nothing about my PTSD or anything about Greg owning a hotel.

Later Greg said he thought they were a couple of shady guys, and we found out later that Giang had met Jeff in the dining room, and Jeff had asked a couple of questions. Giang told him he had a tour and described a little about us.

Later that afternoon, Giang got us a cab, and we headed into Vũng Tàu to an Australian bar called Kelly's Bar. Giang said, "Many Australian veterans moved here to live in Vietnam and mostly hang out here in Vũng Tàu. Many also come during the rainy season because it's cheaper to live here then."

As we drove through the streets, the large homes reminded me of officer billets and the first guard duty I had. I thought it might have been at one of these homes, but I couldn't be sure. On that occasion, I had run into an intruder and laid him out with the butt of my weapon. I always wondered what happened to him, but no one ever said, and I didn't want to ask.

Ky pulled up in front of Kelly's Bar. We got out, walked into the bar, and the owner welcomed us to his establishment. He showed me a book of photos from the War—mostly of Australian soldiers. We enjoyed a couple of beers, but I was disappointed there were no

Australian veterans in the bar. I was looking forward to visiting with them. Later we crossed the street to reach the walkway along the shore. Many fishing boats were tied up for the night. A few fishermen were still swimming with their nets to catch fish.

There was a small park-like area between the sidewalk and road where several Vietnamese men were playing some kind of a ball game, like soccer but different. The walk along the river was enjoyable, watching watercraft transporting people on the river and stopping at various locations such as restaurants and bars. Families were sitting on the rock wall that lined the sidewalk, visiting. There were many vendors parked on the road next to the sidewalk selling various food dishes. Several young ladies had gathered in small groups talking; I guess this area was their social network. Occasionally, there'd be a wink from one of them, a shy smile, etc.; it appeared like more than social networking was planned.

The sun went down, and the town's light took over the beach area. Giang pointed to the restaurant with outdoor seating located on the beach. That restaurant is a great place for dinner," Giang said. The restaurant had a huge outdoor patio, several tables, and lots of staff running around serving the customers. We picked out a table and sat down. It was interesting watching other people—some having dinner with their family; other tables appeared to have business people making deals and raising their glasses in a toast, and at several tables was a young couple having a romantic dinner with candlelight.

We were given a menu and were asked by a young waiter what we'd like to drink. His English was broken and difficult to understand. Giang helped us by translating our dinner and drink orders into Vietnamese. The waiter came up at multiple times to serve; I guessed when a particular dish was ready, it was served.

We could see there was a large group inside having a birthday party celebration. Everyone was enjoying themselves and laughing. There were smaller groups outside having celebrations as well. Next to the restaurant, a large ferry was docking. The sign on the ferry said

Saigon to Vũng Tàu. Many people walked in different directions to the various bars along the pier. Giang said, "as you can see, Vũng Tàu is a hot vacation spot for the Vietnamese, and it shows."

After dinner, we grabbed a cab and headed back to our hotel. The streets were crowded with motorbikes, and sidewalks were jammed-packed with people all having a great time. We arrived at the hotel and decided we would meet for breakfast by 8 a.m. the next day. We would be going back to Saigon. I went to my room, had a hot shower, fixed a drink, packed most things, and did not leave it all for the morning. I sat down, took a drink sip, put my feet up, and leaned back. I thought about the day; it was different from when I was here in 1967. I remembered the white sand on our base was built. Maybe the sand was bleached from the sun; I didn't remember for sure. But I *did* fill a lot of sandbags. Even while I was on guard duty in the city of Vũng Tàu, I didn't see the white sand, only on the base. However, I never made it to the beach, so I didn't know if it had white beaches back then. The one time I *did* have a day pass from the base, we had walked toward town and stopped at the first bar. That was where we spent the day. A short time later, I was transferred to Đồng Tâm.

When I was here during R&R in October 1967, I pretty much hung around the R&R center. They always had entrainment at night with local bands, mostly rock and roll stuff. During the day, I hung out in the nearest bar and visited with other vets. I did sleep a lot which I probably needed; it was a short three days.

CHAPTER 16

Ho Chi Minh City—November 18, 2019

We spent our last full day in Vietnam traveling from Vũng Tàu to Saigon, so it would be easier to catch our flight out in the morning. It was a pleasant drive back. We passed a number of motorbikes, the primary mode of hauling goods to markets. I noticed that a bike had a cage on the back loaded with a number of dogs. "Is this a breeder, Giang?"

Author's Photo Collection
Dogs on the way to dining tables in North Vietnam

"No," he said, half-smiling. "They're going on a trip to Hanoi; dogs are a delicacy there. People generally don't eat dogs here in the south, but in Hanoi and up north, they are in demand by a number of restaurants."

"Oh yuk," Clare said, making a face and turning away.

"If you noticed," said Giang, "you didn't see too many dogs running around; most were tied up or fenced in. The dogs that roam around usually are picked up by the dog runners and hauled to the north."

During the journey, a girl on her motorbike ran into another bike and crashed; not sure what happened to her, but a couple of other motorists immediately stopped to help her, so we just kept going.

"Giang, I have noticed several large sewer pipes along the river. Do they have a system to treat waste?" Greg asked.

At first, Giang looked puzzled. "No system; just pipes are used to route sever to the Mekong delta and then into the ocean and parts beyond.

"I've noticed at least a dozen or more ambulances with red lights going while on this trip," I said. "But one thing I haven't seen are fire engines. Why's that?"

"We don't have many fire engines," Giang said. "Often, they let old homes burn down and rebuild with brick."

I wondered if I was being told a story, so I started paying attention to the houses, and most homes *were* being built with brick or fixed up with a brick. So maybe he was right.

We spent the rest of the drive just enjoying the scenery. The countryside was interesting—a mixture of rice patties and homes scattered between towns or hamlets. I enjoyed seeing the country during a time of peace and not thinking about the past.

"What are your long-term goals, Giang? What do you like to do? I know you said you'd like to be an Ambassador, but I don't think that was very realistic."

"My dream," said Giang, "is to become a lecturer and go to America to inform college students about Vietnam's history and what we are doing to be a free country. I would also like at least one of my kids to move there, get a good education, and have a future. But I'd really like to move my family there and make a life in the 'home of the free,' but that will take some doing. You need to have a sponsor and satisfy a bunch of other requirements."

"I hope you make it someday to America, and I hope you can come to Montana," I said.

"Boy, that would be great," Giang said. "Greg showed me some pictures of rivers that were so clear you could see the rocks along the bottom. I don't know how that can be, but I'd sure like to see that. And the mountains! Greg showed me pictures of what you call Glacier National Park. Now that would be something to see!"

"When you and your family come, I will make sure to be in Montana at the same time. That'll be great to show you around," I said.

Giang's face lit up. "I will look forward to that," he said.

We arrived at the same hotel where this venture all began. Once again, we were met at the door with a welcome by some of the staff. "Have a nice afternoon," Giang said. "We will be here to pick you up and take you to the airport, so see you about 5 a.m."

"Thank you," we said.

"This has been a great tour," I said. "Enjoyed it. See you in the morning." We waved and then turned to go inside.

We checked in again and agreed to meet at the pool in a couple of hours. I dropped my bags, changed my shoes, and decided to walk a little. I needed to stretch my legs. This time I headed off to a different area with more high-end businesses—clothing stores and jewelry stores—where I stopped and browsed. I noticed there weren't any Vietnamese people shopping there—just foreigners. It was strictly for tourists, and I didn't buy anything.

Walking back, I passed several massage places with ladies out front begging passersby to come in and check the place out, but I didn't need to check it out. I already knew what they were selling.

I returned to the hotel, changed, went to the pool, and had a short swim. I ordered a gin and tonic and sat back to relax. Later I met Greg and Clare in the Sky Bar. It had rained lightly, and the air was fresh. It was nice. I looked out over Saigon and said goodbye to Vietnam for the last time.

CHAPTER 17

Ho Chi Minh City–TOKYO–LAX— November 19, 2019

Morning came early, and the restaurant wasn't yet open, so we simply checked out and waited for Giang. He walked in and had a worried look on his face. "I sent Ky a text and reminded him about getting to the airport early this morning. But I haven't heard from him yet."

While we waited for Ky, Greg nodded toward the front desk. I looked over, and a guy with a lady was checking in. She was wearing short shorts, like *really* short shorts, and may as well not have worn anything. "Well, *that's* appropriate," Clare said. "We arrived at this hotel with hookers in the Sky Bar and are leaving with hookers at the front desk."

Greg and I just smiled.

Just as we were about to start worrying about our ride, Ky arrived. We loaded up our bags, crawled into the van, and headed toward the airport. It was just beginning to get daylight as we left, and the traffic was light.

"We really enjoyed this trip," Clare said, "with you as our guide and Ky, our driver. Thank you both for a safe and educational trip!" She gave two envelopes to Giang containing tips that were well-earned.

We drove to the departure area, got out of the car, and unloaded our bags amidst a flurry of hugs and well wishes. With bags in hand, we headed into the terminal. It was easy getting checked in and off to our gate. We had coffee and breakfast at the hospitality club before boarding the plane for the flight home. We had arrived with more than enough time to get to our gate.

The flight to Tokyo seemed short; maybe I was sleeping most of the way. In Tokyo, we had about two hours before our flight to LAX, so we stopped on the way to our connecting gate and did a little shopping. Once airborne again to LAX, the shades on the windows were closed most of the way; most slept. I did spend time thinking about this trip. I knew I needed to take some serious time when I returned home and process it. I needed to answer my questions about my life, image, and nightmares.

We had a snack a few hours before landing and landed at about 9:30 a.m. It was good to get back on American soil. After getting our bags, we got on the shuttle to the hotel, the same one we started the trip with. The rooms weren't ready, so we went to the lounge to relax and discuss the journey. We were overnighted in LA and flew out home the following day.

I was up early. I didn't sleep much as my mind played all the events over the past several days. I met Greg and Clare for breakfast. I think it was one of the better meals on the whole trip.

Clare asked, "Stan, how are you feeling about the trip?"

"Well," I said, "It will take some time. Let it jelly for a couple of months and see if my nightmares and thoughts about life change. I will say the orphanage experience had the biggest effect on me. What were the chances of meeting a nun who was there and remembered most of what happened? I wouldn't have guessed that in a million years. I didn't expect to learn anything about the orphanage. This was quite the trip!"

"It was a great trip," Greg said. "We both enjoyed it and are glad we were with you. It made the trip even more meaningful."

I smiled and nodded. "You know, this trip would not have happened if it wasn't for you two. I can't thank you enough."

My flight to Orlando was at 7 a.m., and they departed for Kalispell soon after. We walked down to the front, saying our good-byes and sharing some hugs, and I loaded up on the shuttle.

It was nice to get home. I am getting back to some everyday life and thinking about the past several days. I owned it to myself to take some quiet time and address the effects of this trip. I know God determines the answer to many questions, and we live the life He chooses. We just have to live that life, knowing there is a reason for everything.

EPILOGUE

When I was waiting to board the aircraft in Saigon in July 1968, following my thirteen-month tour of duty in Vietnam, the last thing I would have expected was to come back to that place. For many years, I didn't acknowledge to anyone that I was a Vietnam Vet, and even if someone asked, I would quickly change the subject. Vietnam Veterans were not treated well, and even now, I still hear criticism of veterans from that war, although it is much less common than it was back then.

Over the next forty-plus years, I apparently seemed normal to most people, even though my insides were often in turmoil. Not until forty-five years after the Vietnam War ended was I diagnosed with PTSD, and I learned that the feelings I had been hiding were normal for people living with PTSD.

It wasn't until I wrote my book, *You Are Never Alone*, that I started to handle better my daily images, nightly dreams, and nightmares. It was about that time I began thinking about the possibility of returning to Vietnam to face my demons, but I knew the only way that could happen would be by some miracle.

When Greg said, "We're going to Vietnam," and explained his reasons for the trip, I thought how lucky I was to have a cousin who would make this possible for me. Greg and I indeed had a lot in common—our families had camped together and celebrated events together; we had both found work as contractors and taken up scuba diving together—but for *anyone* to spend several thousand dollars on me for the trip of a lifetime was really special. I understood how Greg felt about his dad and what he had gone through during World War II. My mom had told me several times about what his dad had experienced, and it was clear that fighting in the Philippines and New Guinea in the 1940s was no cakewalk either. Greg believed that his father might have benefited from a return to those places that had stolen his innocence and forever changed him, but that was not to be. As it turned out, his loss was my unexpected gain.

Now, nearly ten months after taking that trip, I still think about many things that happened during the War and how things had changed during the intervening years. But meeting a VC soldier during peacetime, making friends with several very gracious Vietnamese people, and having a knowledgeable tour guide was more than I had expected. I am grateful to all of them. But what specifically helped me most about the trip boils down to this: The best way for me to address my PTSD is to separately tackle each trauma that feeds my nightmares and my three daily images.

First, there was Stewart, who died in my arms. I could not let that go and blamed myself every day since that tragic event. Why was it him and not me? How does God choose who dies and who lives in war? Stewart had a family and two beautiful daughters, while I was neither married nor did I have children. In my way of thinking about the event, it clearly should have been me who should have suffered from the explosion. We were only a few feet apart, but God spared me for some reason. I still think about it, and during our trip to Đồng Tâm, I was disappointed that we weren't allowed to enter the base. It would have been nice to see that again and perhaps put some closure to that particular image. During the flight home, I reflected on that event and had to admit that some soldiers died, and there was no rhyme or reason for who was chosen. On that particular day, in that specific year, and during that particular war, Stewart was the chosen one, and my role was to make sure he didn't die alone, and I was there for his last moments to give him comfort. That was my job.

Second, there was the NVA soldier who I'm sure I killed during an ambush. I was told to check him for intel, and I found a photograph of his young wife and baby in his chest pocket. The recurring image of this incident is the small black-and-white picture. It's not the soldier who returns in my vision; it's the baby. At the time, I felt I had killed a husband, father, and a dad—a human being—not a soldier. When the Sargent asked me what I found, I told him what I thought. He quickly reminded me that I could have been lying there with him going through *my* stuff. I understand, at least rationally, that it's not about the soldier. But my dream, and remorse, are about the baby. Did it grow up? Do they know what happened? Did they grow up to have a family of their own? Or maybe they didn't even live through the war. The image was just a reminder of War, and I am no longer as stressed about it—maybe because of my visit with the school girl in the market who told me the new generation of Vietnamese children has a promising future. That provided me with some solace and some peace.

My third image was the one that had the most significant effect on me and resulted in the belief that I was not worthy of fathering a child—a decision I have lived to regret. In 1967, while stationed in Đồng Tâm, I made several visits to the orphanage in Mỹ Tho. I was drawn to the innocence of the children and their simple joy at having an adult spend time playing games with them, despite the lack of a common language. Two of the children—a young boy and a girl—stole my heart. My first book, *You Are Never Alone*, provides a chapter entitled "My Worst Fears" and details my relationship with those children who ultimately died due to an act of the enemy—an act which I brought to an end. This event haunted me for fifty-four years. My main goal during our return trip to Vietnam was to find this orphanage and find someone or something that would help bring some closure to this chapter in my life. The day I met Sister

Renee—the last of the nuns who lived at the orphanage during the attack—was when I began to heal. What were the odds of finding one of the last people alive who knew of the incident in the courtyard and had been friends with the nun who was killed on that fateful day? By spending several hours visiting Sister Renee, I finally found some peace. I realized that spending time with the orphan children, and mainly the two I had developed a close friendship with, had brought joy to their lives as much as to mine. And when the time came to spare them from the tortures of war, I was there to bring them peace.

The return trip to Vietnam was an invaluable healing experience, and I will be forever grateful to those who contributed time, energy, and funds to make that trip a reality. My Vietnam experience has dominated my life for over half a century, and now I believe it may be time, at last, to put that experience on the road to rest.

APPENDIX

Background History of Vietnam—The Country

This entry aims to give the reader who does not have firsthand experience of Vietnam a general overview of the country, climate, culture, history, and related information. The following are extracts from Vietnam Country Dossier prepared by Audley travel, along with my personal experience. In other places, I inserted information about various locations to give the reader a better understanding of the location and its history.

Geography—Vietnam is a country of beauty with many unspoiled beaches, mist-shrouded mountains, brilliant green rice paddies, and tropical rainforests. It shares borders to the north with China and the west with Laos and Cambodia. The south China Sea lies to the east and south.

Climate—Vietnam is a land of many contrasts, and its weather is one of those. The country is divided into northern, central, and southern regions.

The northern region has a cool, dry climate from October through March. April begins to warm up, and showers are expected. June to September tends to be hot and humid with tropical rains. The mountainous areas tend to be even cooler and may require warmer clothing.

The central areas experience rain for a large part of the year. The weather's hot and sunny from June to August.

The south of Vietnam is best visited from November to May. The remaining months are hot, humid, and generally wet conditions.

Entry and Health—Vietnam requires Visas and is suitable for one month for single-entry tourists. Longer duration for business and multiple entry visas can also be arranged. A valid passport is also required.

Standard vaccinations are advisable for diphtheria, tetanus, polio, typhoid, and hepatitis A. Also, check with your local US health clinic for other requirements.

Currency—Vietnam money is in Dong. Before leaving, I purchased approximately $300 US worth of Dong, about 6.95 million Dong from my local Wells Fargo bank, and the ATMs took care of the remaining needs throughout Vietnam. Dong comes in various denominations, and I found anything over 100,000 Dong was hard or impossible to use in smaller shops. I carried most of my dong in 500,000 bills and had 200,000 in smaller bills; 10,000, 20,000, 50,000, and 100,000 work great. I would stop at the local bank if I needed to change 500,000 into smaller bills. Also, many places accepted US currency. One caution: do not write on money or tear them as they will not be accepted or exchanged.

Tipping is as much a part of Vietnamese culture as in any country. It would be best if you were prepared to tip your guides, drivers, porters, and servers. There are guidelines from your travel coordinator. I did find charitable organizations that ran a couple of restaurants we visited, and servers were not allowed to accept tips.

Safety/Security—Vietnam is a safe country to travel in. Petty crime is your greatest worry. I have included an incident we encountered in the book. Most hotels will have a safe in your room or available at the main desk. I made it a practice to keep my money on me in a secure pocket or my safe in the room. You will need your passport to check in at the hotel, but keep your travel documents in a safe place and carry copies with you.

History—Vietnam's history is fascinating, stretching over thousands of years and dominated by many conflicts.

Early years, Vietnam was under Chinese rule until early in the tenth century; Vietnam was under the control of the Portuguese, French, and several other countries even after it obtained independence. Their history is littered with occupations from other countries. The US soldiers went home when they met their objectives based on the Paris Agreement. However, up to 300,000 South Vietnamese, including our guide, were sent to re-education camps, where many endured torture, starvation, and disease while being forced to perform hard labor. The New Economic Zones program was implemented by the Vietnamese Communist Government after the Fall of Saigon. Between 1975 and 1980, more than one million Northerners migrated to the south and central regions, formerly under the Republic of Vietnam. This program, in turn, displaced around 750,000 to over 1 million Southerners from their homes and forcibly relocated them to uninhabited mountainous, forested areas.

Compounding economic difficulties were new military challenges. In the late 1970s, Cambodia started harassing and raiding Vietnamese villages at the shared border under the Khmer Rouge regime. To neutralize the threat, the People's Army of Vietnam invaded Cambodia in 1978 and overran its capital Phnom Penh, driving out the incumbent Khmer Rouge regime. In response, as an action to support the pro-Beijing Khmer Rouge regime, China increased its pressure on Vietnam and sent troops into Northern Vietnam in 1979 to "punish" Vietnam. Relations between the two countries had been deteriorating for some time. Territorial disagreements along the border and in the South China Sea that had remained dormant during the Vietnam War were revived at the War's end. A postwar campaign engineered by Hanoi against the ethnic Chinese Hoa community elicited a strong protest from Beijing. China was displeased with Vietnam's alliance with the Soviet Union. During its prolonged military occupation of Cambodia from 1979–1989, Vietnam's international isolation extended to relations with the United States. The United States, in addition to citing Vietnam's minimal cooperation in accounting for Americans who were missing in action (MIAs) as an obstacle to normal relations, barred regular ties as long as Vietnamese troops occupied Cambodia. Washington also continued to enforce the trade embargo imposed on Hanoi after the war in 1975. If you're interested in more detail about Vietnamese history, many reports, books, and studies are available on the Internet.

REFERENCES

https://www2.gwu.edu/~erpapers/mep/displaydoc.cfm?docid=er-pn-henlod Cabot Lodge

https://www.history.com/this-day-in-history/north-vietnamese-launch-ho-chi-minh-campaign

https://www.history.com/this-day-in-history/operation-baby-lift-concludes

https://www.history.com/this-day-in-history/south-vietnam-surrenders

https://www.history.com/this-day-in-history/u-s-withdraws-from-vietnam

https://www.britannica.com/place/Vietnam/BenTri

https://www.britannica.com/place/My-Tho

https://wikitravel.org/en/Can_Tho

https://www.historynet.com/vung-tau-vietnams-hottest-rr-destination.htm

https://www.history.com/this-day-in-history/paris-peace-accords-signed

https://en.wikipedia.org/wiki/Caravelle_Hotel

https://www.history.com/topics/vietnam-war/tet-offensive

https://www.npr.org/transcripts/102373662 Monks and PTSD

https://www.ncbi.nlm.nih.gov/pmc/articles/PMC5299042/ VC/NVA PTSD

CPSIA information can be obtained
at www.ICGtesting.com
Printed in the USA
LVHW051930310323
743160LV00009B/220

9 781959 493747